NUTRITION
FOR INTUITION

ALSO BY DOREEN VIRTUE AND ROBERT REEVES, N.D.

Books

Living Pain-Free
Angel Detox
Flower Therapy

Card Deck

Flower Therapy Oracle Cards

ALSO BY DOREEN VIRTUE

Books/Calendars/Kits/Oracle Board

10 Messages Your Angels Want You to Know (available November 2016)
Veggie Momma (with Jenny Ross; available September 2016)
Awaken Your Indigo Power (with Charles Virtue; available August 2016)
The Courage to Be Creative (available June 2016)
Don't Let Anything Dull Your Sparkle
2016 Angel Engagement Calendar
Angel Affirmations 2016 Calendar
Earth Angel Realms
The Big Book of Angel Tarot (with Radleigh Valentine)
Angels of Abundance (with Grant Virtue)
Angel Dreams (with Melissa Virtue)
Angel Astrology 101 (with Yasmin Boland)
Assertiveness for Earth Angels
How to Heal a Grieving Heart (with James Van Praagh)
The Essential Doreen Virtue Collection
The Miracles of Archangel Gabriel
Mermaids 101
Mary, Queen of Angels
Saved by an Angel
The Angel Therapy® Handbook
Angel Words (with Grant Virtue)
Archangels 101
The Healing Miracles of Archangel Raphael
The Art of Raw Living Food (with Jenny Ross)
Signs from Above (with Charles Virtue)
The Miracles of Archangel Michael
Angel Numbers 101
Solomon's Angels (a novel)
My Guardian Angel (with Amy Oscar)

Angel Blessings Candle Kit (with Grant Virtue; includes booklet, CD, journal, etc.)

Thank You, Angels! (children's book with Kristina Tracy)

Healing Words from the Angels

How to Hear Your Angels

Fairies 101

Daily Guidance from Your Angels

Divine Magic

How to Give an Angel Card Reading Kit

Angels 101

Angel Guidance Board

Crystal Therapy (with Judith Lukomski)

Connecting with Your Angels Kit (includes booklet, CD, journal, etc.)

The Crystal Children

Archangels & Ascended Masters

Earth Angels

Messages from Your Angels

Angel Visions II

Eating in the Light (with Becky Black, M.F.T., R.D.)

The Care and Feeding of Indigo Children

Angel Visions

Divine Prescriptions

Healing with the Angels

"I'd Change My Life If I Had More Time"

Divine Guidance

Chakra Clearing

Angel Therapy®

Constant Craving A–Z

Constant Craving

The Yo-Yo Diet Syndrome

Losing Your Pounds of Pain

Audio/CD Programs

The Healing Miracles of Archangel Raphael
(unabridged audio book)

Angel Therapy® Meditations

Archangels 101 (abridged audio book)

Solomon's Angels (unabridged audio book)

Fairies 101 (abridged audio book)

Angel Medicine (available as both 1- and 2-CD sets)

Angels among Us (with Michael Toms)

Messages from Your Angels (abridged audio book)

Past-Life Regression with the Angels

Divine Prescriptions

The Romance Angels

Connecting with Your Angels

Manifesting with the Angels

Karma Releasing
Healing Your Appetite, Healing Your Life
Healing with the Angels
Divine Guidance
Chakra Clearing

DVD Program

How to Give an Angel Card Reading

Card Decks

Butterfly Oracle Cards for Life Changes (available May 2016)
Loving Words from Jesus (available March 2016)
Archangel Gabriel Oracle Cards
Fairy Tarot Cards (with Radleigh Valentine)
Angel Answers Oracle Cards (with Radleigh Valentine)
Past Life Oracle Cards (with Brian Weiss, M.D.)
Guardian Angel Tarot Cards (with Radleigh Valentine)
Cherub Angel Cards for Children
Talking to Heaven Mediumship Cards
(with James Van Praagh)
Archangel Power Tarot Cards (with Radleigh Valentine)
Indigo Angel Oracle Cards (with Charles Virtue)
Angel Dreams Oracle Cards (with Melissa Virtue)
Mary, Queen of Angels Oracle Cards
Angel Tarot Cards (with Radleigh Valentine
and Steve A. Roberts)
The Romance Angels Oracle Cards
Life Purpose Oracle Cards
Archangel Raphael Healing Oracle Cards
Archangel Michael Oracle Cards
Angel Therapy® Oracle Cards
Magical Messages from the Fairies Oracle Cards
Ascended Masters Oracle Cards
Daily Guidance from Your Angels Oracle Cards
Saints & Angels Oracle Cards
Magical Unicorns Oracle Cards
Goddess Guidance Oracle Cards
Archangel Oracle Cards
Magical Mermaids and Dolphins Oracle Cards
Messages from Your Angels Oracle Cards
Healing with the Fairies Oracle Cards
Healing with the Angels Oracle Cards

All of the above are available at your local bookstore, or may be ordered by visiting:
Hay House USA: www.hayhouse.com®; Hay House Australia: www.hayhouse.com.au;
Hay House UK: www.hayhouse.co.uk; Hay House South Africa: www.hayhouse.co.za;
Hay House India: www.hayhouseco.in

Doreen's website: www.AngelTherapy.com

NUTRITION
FOR INTUITION

DOREEN VIRTUE AND
ROBERT REEVES, N.D.

HAY HOUSE, INC.
Carlsbad, California • New York City
London • Sydney • Johannesburg
Vancouver • Hong Kong • New Delhi

Published and distributed in the United States by: Hay House, Inc.: www.hayhouse
.com® • *Published and distributed in Australia by:* Hay House Australia Pty. Ltd.: www
.hayhouse.com.au • *Published and distributed in the United Kingdom by:* Hay House
UK, Ltd.: www.hayhouse.co.uk • *Published and distributed in the Republic of South
Africa by:* Hay House SA (Pty), Ltd.: www.hayhouse.co.za • *Distributed in Canada by:*
Raincoast Books: www.raincoast.com • *Published in India by:* Hay House Publishers
India: www.hayhouse.co.in

Cover design: Amy Rose Grigoriou • *Interior design:* Pamela Homan • *Illustrations:* Page
14: Negovura/Shutterstock modified by Doreen Virtue and Robert Reeves, N.D. • Page
35: D. Czarnota/Shutterstock modified by Doreen Virtue and Robert Reeves, N.D.

Library of Congress Cataloging-in-Publication Data

Virtue, Doreen, date, author.
  Nutrition for intuition / Doreen Virtue and Robert Reeves, N.D.
      pages cm
    Includes bibliographical references.
    ISBN 978-1-4019-4541-1 (paperback)
  1. Mental healing. 2. Mind and body--Health aspects. 3. Nutrition. 4. Spiritual healing. I. Reeves, Robert (Naturopath) II. Title.
    RZ400.V55 2016
    615.8'528--dc23

                                2015029860

ISBN: 978-1-4019-4541-1

10 9 8 7 6 5 4 3 2
1st edition, January 2016

Printed in the United States of America

To you,
for having the courage
to awaken your natural
intuitive abilities

CONTENTS

INTRODUCTION

Intuition is a natural skill we all possess, similar to our ability to breathe, speak, or see. At one time, it was considered a myth. Today, it is scientifically confirmed.

One of the leading researchers on the topic of intuition, John Bargh of Yale University, says that our brains use unconscious automatic processes—which he terms "automaticity"—to instantly evaluate and immediately apprehend our surroundings, with effects that are prevalent throughout our lives.

Even so, intuition is not necessarily the go-to operating mode for everyone. A highly respected psychometric test called the *Myers-Briggs Type Indicator personality inventory* helps people pinpoint whether their natural tendency is more "intuitive" or "sensory":

- **Intuitive** people tend to read between the lines, look for signs, and heed their inner signals when making decisions.

- Those who are **sensory** use their heads more than their hearts, and they focus upon facts, figures, and what they can tangibly measure and define.

In other words, naturally intuitive people are more "inner focused" on their own impressions and feelings, and sensory people are focused on the outer world of what they can physically feel, see, and hear, and can analyze logically.

Yet, after teaching psychic-development classes to thousands of people—men and women, young and old—worldwide since 1995, I (Doreen) firmly believe that intuition is an innate faculty *anyone* can develop. We all have the capacity for intuition, and some have already practiced it to different degrees.

Intuition is a valuable resource, yet if yours seems sporadic or hazy, this book can help you enjoy more consistency and clarity. Additionally, if you struggle to receive intuitive information, your diet may be blocking you. You can add foods and drinks to your lifestyle that will increase your intuition and spiritual awareness.

Here are our personal stories of how changing our diets improved our intuition—and our lives. . . .

Doreen's Story

Like many children, I was born with my clairvoyance wide-open. In fact, I've had visions my entire life. However, although the visions were pleasant, I didn't understand or welcome them. I tried to consciously shut down my intuition since I was highly sensitive and could feel everyone's emotions. The bombarding energies were overwhelming.

If this weren't enough, when I grew older and prayed for my Divine life purpose to be revealed, I had visions of writing books and speaking in front of audiences and on television. These visions intimidated me! I loved writing, but I wondered, *How do you get published and on TV?* And what would I write *about?* I wanted a more accessible life purpose, but the visions continued, with the message that I was supposed to write about spirituality. . . .

That is, until my visions and intuition began to *dim.*

The more I ate ice cream and other junk food, the less sensitive I was. I gained weight, but the payoff was that the visions stopped.

Then one night when my family was asleep upstairs, I grabbed a carton of ice cream and sat in front of the TV set. Before I could pick up the spoon, the message came to take a good look at what I was about to do. This gentle confrontation helped me see just how unhealthily and unlovingly I was treating myself. I put down the ice cream and got on my knees. I said to God, "I don't know how to put these visions into action! I will surrender to Your will, but I'm frightened."

That was the night that my whole life changed. The next day, following my guidance (without any junk food in my stomach), I enrolled in the local community college. I applied for and received a student loan to pay for my tuition and expenses. As guided, I took college courses on psychology part-time over the next decade, while working full-time as a secretary.

My first job as a therapist was a volunteer position at an inpatient hospital treating drug addicts and alcoholics. Within four months, I was hired full-time and was able to leave my secretarial position. I continued college in the evenings.

At the hospital, I audited some group therapy sessions for people who had eating disorders. I instantly fell in love with eating-disorder counseling and left the hospital position to work at an outpatient clinic. The supervising therapist supported me in opening a private practice specializing in treating compulsive overeating, bulimia, and anorexia. My practice thrived, and I continued doing research with my clients, attending conferences, and poring over scientific journal articles.

I wrote several books about food and healing from eating disorders.

Then, in 1996, I began having visions of food.

While meditating, in my mind's eye, I could see images of what I commonly ate. It wasn't a conjuring image, like when you're hungry. These were spontaneous visuals of food, appearing as three-dimensional objects.

I had no idea why I was seeing this. It took me several months to realize that my food visions were answers to the question I'd asked of God about how to increase my visual intuition.

What I learned from my scientific research—and from the visions—is that there are foods that turn *off* intuition and others that turn it *on.*

I followed this visual guidance and changed my diet. Almost immediately, my visions vastly improved. It was like upgrading from a tiny television set to a high-definition large-screen! Suddenly, my visions were fully formed and more understandable.

Again following my guidance, I began teaching classes to help others awaken their spiritual abilities to see and feel guidance. I taught my students about the connection between food and intuition, and many of them changed their diets, with outcomes similar to the one I'd had. I also appeared on TV Food Network frequently, discussing the links between emotions and food, as well as other television and radio shows.

This book is the result of all these experiences and my research, coupled with the expertise of my friend and co-author Robert Reeves, an Australian naturopath. Robert's own studies and work have specialized in blending natural and spiritual healing methods, and he openly combines his intuitive work with his naturopathy. He has been successful in helping many people and enjoys a busy practice.

Here is Robert's story about food and intuition. . . .

Robert's Story

I began exploring spirituality at a young age. Something within me was fascinated by the topics of intuition and energetic healing. So, following my guidance, I began attending spiritual workshops at just 14. Naturally, I was the youngest person there . . . and one of only a handful of males! Most spiritual seminars at the time were filled with audiences of women. Luckily for me, these loving "mothers" happily adopted me for the weekend workshops. It allowed me to feel safe and comfortable—the perfect setting to connect with my intuition!

I practiced meditating regularly, working with oracle cards, and giving healings. I felt strongly connected to my angels and was confident in my ability to understand their messages.

A few years went by and I turned 18—which is the legal age for drinking alcohol in Australia. I suppose the "normal" thing to do when you come of age would be to have a big party and get drunk. Well, that's not exactly what I did. I did have a big party with all my friends, which I catered with secretly vegetarian food. There were pretend sausages and fake bacon (some of which perhaps weren't as convincing as I thought), as well as fresh juices. Since I wasn't (and still am not) interested in drinking alcohol at all, I didn't have a single drop.

Despite my aversion to the nightlife scene, my friends still dragged me out to clubs from time to time. I went along with it because I already felt different enough and didn't want to be missing out. We hung out, my friends drank, and I was the driver. One night we grabbed some fast food before heading home, and as I ate, I felt a little strange. I couldn't quite put my finger on it, but I just wasn't myself.

When I woke up the next morning, I felt like I had a hangover! I was the only person who didn't drink any alcohol, yet I awoke with a splitting headache. It didn't make any sense. I suspected it was just the horrible energy of the clubs, but it felt like there was more to it.

That day, I felt more distracted, restless, and unfocused. When I tried to connect with God and the angels, it was more difficult than usual. I could sense my angels with me, yet I couldn't understand what guidance they were trying to give me. I'd worked so hard to build my intuition, and it felt like I'd taken ten steps backward in one night. So right then and there I made the decision to only go to places that felt positive and happy.

A few weeks went by and I caught up with some friends for lunch. We met at a fast-food place and enjoyed a good chat while we ate. Later in the afternoon I was back home doing some gardening. I love being outdoors in nature and surrounded by healing flowers. All of a sudden I started to feel a headache coming on. It felt very similar to the "hangover" headache from a few weeks earlier.

I put my hands on either side of my head as I silently asked, *What's going on?* I could feel my angels with me, but the lines of communication seemed clouded again. So I sat on the grass, closed my eyes, and breathed.

Then I heard, *It's the fast food.*

My eyes flew open with shock, as I'd never even considered that. Unhealthy food was blocking my intuition and preventing me from hearing my angels!

From that point on, I've taken note of how I feel when I try new foods. *Do I feel more open and connected? Or do I feel tired, unmotivated, and separated?* These simple questions have helped me find the right foods for my body and energy. I've now come to fully understand that what you eat really *does* have a powerful impact on your intuitive abilities.

About This Book

In this book, you'll learn what to eat and what to avoid, in order to augment your spiritual gifts of intuition and clairvoyance. We'll also help you learn how to manage your intuition so that you're not overwhelmed with feelings and messages.

Although there have been previous writings about how foods can increase intuition, they mostly were limited to recommending that you match the colors of your foods to the colors of your chakras. In other words, they were recommending a plant-based diet with a rainbow of food colors—for example, eat a red apple to increase the energy of your red root chakra, and so forth. While it's helpful to consume colorful fruits and vegetables, *Nutrition for Intuition* covers more specifics because you need a deeper understanding of nutrition to supply your body with the full range of nutrients it needs.

"Nutrition" doesn't just mean our diet, however. It really refers to our lifestyle and the way in which it affects whether we can clearly receive Divine messages. So, this book discusses foods, but it also touches on so much more:

- In **Part I**, we explain how intuition works; the energy centers and physiology underlying clairsentience, clairvoyance, clairaudience, and claircognizance; and the link to nutrition.

- **Part II** offers general advice on how to eat and honor your uniqueness, along with specific foods, liquids, and herbs to enhance your intuitive abilities.

- Finally, in **Part III**, we discuss the power of detoxing and chakra-clearing methods to keep your energy high, as well as how to call upon the angels for help in changing your lifestyle. (In addition, we have included an **Appendix** in the back of the book with further information on the chakras, plus a handy chart summarizing the food recommendations to support your individual "clairs" and a glossary of nutritional supplements.)

Our intention is to give you every available tool so that you can clearly understand the messages you're receiving from God and your Higher Self.

You Already *Are* Intuitive

You have natural intuitive abilities. In fact, science demonstrates that we *all* inherently do. And yet, if you struggle to connect with the Divine, your diet could be a culprit. By making some shifts in what you eat and drink, you can allow your inner intuitive light to shine more brightly.

I (Doreen) had profound positive changes in my intuitive and clairvoyant abilities when I listened to my inner guidance and made dietary changes. At first, I resisted these changes. But when I finally made the shift, the rewards were worth it!

This book is a culmination of our personal experiences, guidance we've received during readings, and feedback from our workshop participants. There's no one method of eating that's going to suit everyone, and we aren't trying to suggest that with this book. Instead, *Nutrition for Intuition* brings together the nutrition/intuition research that we've gathered over the years, based upon clinical and personal discoveries, along with medical and psychological studies.

When our clients have adopted a certain way of approaching food, positive shifts have occurred. We want to share these concepts—and a few recipes—which we know will help you in your quest for greater intuition. Embrace the changes that you feel guided to make, try some new things, and allow God and your angels to help you along the way.

With love and respect,
Doreen and Robert

An Important Note

Within this book we share nutritional information about foods, herbs, and supplements. Please note that the suggestions and dosages may or may not be appropriate for you. Please check with your physician/health-care professional, therapist, or dietitian prior to starting any new health regimen.

PART I

The Nutrition–Intuition Connection

CHAPTER ONE

The Physiology of Intuition

Every single one of us will experience our intuition differently. That's why reading a book on the meanings of symbols can sometimes be misleading. While those symbols are relevant for that particular author, for you the signs that come up through your intuition may be completely different.

There are many different definitions of *intuition,* as what constitutes intuition to one person does not look the same to another. Some people recognize it as a connection with God and their guardian angels. For others, it's simply a gut feeling or an inner knowingness about what they need to do. For others still, it's the guidance received during psychic readings. All of these definitions are accurate, and appropriate for the individuals in question.

Now, that doesn't mean that certain people are more or less intuitive. Rather, it's simply a difference in style that needs to be acknowledged. When you realize that your abilities are just as powerful as the next person's, you're able to let go of the need to compare yourself to someone else. You then realize that your intuition is perfectly attuned to *you.*

In order to explain what intuition is in the most inclusive way, we've called upon heavenly assistance. We've asked our angels to share *their* definition with you.

They say:

"Intuition is your ability to receive and interpret Divine healing and supportive messages for your journey. It gives you the clarity to know that you are going in the right direction, and to understand what changes you need to make in your life."

In essence, your intuition is the Divine connection that you have to the angels, Spirit, the Universe, and our Creator. It is that "telephone line" to Source. As you fine-tune your intuitive gifts, you're able to more easily recognize what Heaven is trying to tell you.

The whispers from God and the angels that you hear in moments of calmness and tranquility *are* your intuition. You can understand, then, how it is much easier to tap into it when you're feeling relaxed and at peace. It's a very different story if you go to the shopping mall on Christmas Eve. At that moment so many different energies are rushing around you. People are getting caught up in stress and anxiety and a great deal of fear. In that moment your intuition hasn't gone away; it's just become more challenging to hear.

As we teach you everything we've learned over our many years of connecting with God and the angels and being conscious of our health, you'll start to see that certain choices you make regarding your lifestyle and diet can dramatically enhance your intuitive gifts. You'll truly be able to connect with God and your angels—even on Christmas Eve at the shopping mall.

Remember that when your life doesn't look the way you want it to, you have the power to change that. You have the ability to shape and create your reality, because what you do causes a ripple effect of change across the Universe. Whether or not you realize it, the Universe is reacting to every single step you take. It's viewed as a very deliberate and conscious action on your part.

Ask yourself the questions *In what direction did I go with my last step? In what direction am I heading?* If your surroundings are unlike the vision you have for your future, then let's choose to walk in another direction. Let's take the next step toward your goals rather than toward fear.

Your intuition is unique to you. It's something that you need to honor and learn to trust. Start off by focusing on the small steps you feel directed to take so that when your intuition hits you with big, life-changing, transformative guidance, you won't even hesitate.

Throughout this book we're going to give you suggestions for foods that will help keep your intuitive feelings switched on all the time, because we believe that living a life according to your guidance is always going to lead you down a path of greater joy and well-being.

Trusting Your Intuition

You might ask why your intuition isn't already fully activated. Well, this could be for a number of reasons. It may be due to your conditioning (the way in which your family behaved), the culture you were raised in, or just society in general. Your personality could also be a factor. If you are naturally a sensory, "outer-focused" person, you may stuff down or dismiss your intuition because you question what you can't explain logically.

If your family holds certain religious beliefs, then you may have been taught that it was wrong to trust your gut feelings. Perhaps you were instructed not to express yourself—especially if your ideas and views were different from everybody else's. Maybe your culture encouraged you to believe that it's dangerous to embrace your psychic abilities.

Society is constantly changing and evolving, and for a period of time, the cultural tide had turned against trusting our gut feelings. We were told that everything needed to be scientifically proven, with clear results from clinical trials and medical studies, to show us the valid choices for living our lives.

Thankfully, society is beginning to change, and we're seeing that our intuitive and spiritual gifts are once again being celebrated.

Practical Intuition

Our intuition is an inner voice that speaks with an essence of love. As we connect to that loving energy, we feel supported. We feel relaxed and safe, knowing that everything happening at this moment has a greater purpose.

Begin with those small calls to action, the ones that say, *Today reach to out your friend*—because who knows what that friend is going through at this moment. Understand that those gut feelings, and that sense of urgency behind them, may very well be lifesaving for that dear loved one of yours.

If you "hold on" to that intuitive guidance, it's like a mail carrier receiving a parcel and refusing to deliver it. If you keep it to yourself, only *one* person is going to benefit from it, and that's you. However, if you choose to share that message—to have the courage and the confidence to speak what you feel—then it may change the lives of your loved ones and allow *them* to feel happier and freer . . . and be inspired to then trust their own gut feelings. They, in turn, will share *their* intuitive messages, and that ripple effect spreads.

As you listen to your inner guidance, it may tell you something simple, such as *Switch lanes,* while you're driving in the car. It may become more complex, such as *You need to leave that relationship, You need to change careers,* or *You need to move.*

Your intuition can be like an internal lie detector. When you meet someone, you can immediately tell if you like him or her or if something about what he or she is saying rings untrue. You get a sense of somebody's energy the instant that you make a connection, and your internal lie detector says, *Yes, this is a wonderful person!*—or, it does the opposite and tells you to get as far away as you possibly can.

Sometimes you pick up on different energies when you're in somebody's home. Do you feel uplifted, or do you get a sense that the person is just trying to impress you? Is that energy stagnant with negativity? You'll know.

So please trust the messages that you receive when you meet somebody or when you enter a new environment. Do so especially if you're going to see practitioners or healers, because if you go into a space feeling uncertain or afraid, that's a sign to step back.

This is something that we've learned to listen to when we've been invited to attend particular seminars. We feel that our purpose here on Earth is to help as many people as we can. We hope to spread healing messages about spirituality, natural health, God, and the angels. But we still have to trust our own intuition. Sometimes we get invited to speak at events that sound wonderful, but there's something in our gut that says, *Don't do it.*

When we trust that information, even though it might feel uncomfortable at the time, we're then able to look back on that event at a later date and understand why we were guided to stay away. Often it's not because the organizers or attendees were "bad" or anything like that, but rather something else came up that more urgently required our attention. We might not have been able to give 100 percent at that particular event. Perhaps we'd been so busy throughout the year that we needed some time to rest.

As you listen to your intuition, you learn that the way in which God and your angels communicate with you is special and unique because *you* are special and unique. Rather than feeling like you have to fit inside a box, honor your own perceptions.

Trust your intuition. Truly, it's the heavenly voice of God and your angels coming through.

Science and Intuition

At one time, intuition was considered an old wives' tale. Today, researchers have solid scientific foundations for the process of intuition. Dozens of studies support the value of intuition in decision making and finding creative solutions to problems. A recent study concluded that medical doctors can achieve better outcomes in their patients' care by calling upon their intuition. The researchers stated, "Intuitive and analytical decision processes may have complementary effects in achieving the desired outcomes of patient decision support" (de Vries et al. 2013). A related study found that farmers use intuition *more* than analytics.

Many studies have focused on our physical reactions to various situations, measuring blood pressure, brain waves, perspiration, and heart rate in response to stimuli, such as looking at emotionally charged photos or video clips. In some intriguing experiments, the participants' heart and other systems were shown to react to a photo or video even *before* the people being studied were exposed to the stimulus. Most of these experiments are "double-blind," which means that neither the participants nor the researchers know beforehand which type of image the person being studied will see. The studies show that our bodies "know" when something emotionally charged is coming our way.

Perhaps you've had this experience yourself, when you woke up feeling excited or happy for no known reason. Or, similarly, you felt a sense of dread on a day when something unforeseen and unpleasant later occurred.

Research has demonstrated that our palms begin to sweat when we're around something harsh or dangerous several minutes *before* our conscious minds can register the threat. This makes sense, as the hands have a high number of sensory neuronal connections to the nervous system. Scientists believe that if we could learn to pay attention to our palms' subtle signals, including perspiration, it would enable us to be consciously aware of—and avoid—danger.

Similar studies find that our heart rate and blood pressure increase when people are directing negative thoughts our way, and that these functions relax and decrease when others are thinking positive thoughts about us. It turns out that "sending love" is a measurable energy!

Intuition Works with the Body's Systems

Our ancient ancestors relied on their intuition to ensure their physical safety. Imagine the vulnerable feeling of walking outside to forage for food, where you depend on your wits to stay alive. This is the same built-in system wild animals use for survival. While we now shop in grocery stores for food and live in houses, this doesn't mean that our ancestors' instincts have "evolved away."

Researchers have pinpointed the brain's right hemisphere, which is associated with emotions and the arts, as the center of our intuition. Additionally, the autonomic nervous system, also called our "ancient brain," appears to be hardwired to instinctively react to potential danger in a way that could be called "intuitive." The brain's limbic system—our feeling center—can sense danger detected by the autonomic nervous system before it's physically apparent. In this way, our intuition (if we listen to it) keeps us safe.

In the face of stress, our nervous and endocrine systems work closely together to bring about harmony and balance. These two systems are linked by the hypothalamus, a structure in the brain's limbic system. While the endocrine system is made up of many glands, the most important with a bearing on stress and intuition are the pituitary and adrenal glands. Let's look at how all these systems work together.

When your nervous system recognizes a stressor, it sends a message to the hypothalamus, which releases hormones to deliver the message to the pituitary gland. Next, the pituitary sends out hormones influencing the adrenal glands. In turn, this causes your adrenals to release a hormone to reduce the effects of the stress. This pattern continues until your body is satisfied that you have enough stress-relieving hormones available. Your body then relaxes, and the nervous system calms.

However, if stress continues for extended periods of time, the biological exchange of neuro-messages and hormones may become unbalanced. If the hypothalamus, pituitary, or adrenal glands become depleted, it creates a strain along the cascade. This causes a change in your stress response, energy levels, and hormones.

By supporting your endocrine and nervous systems nutritionally, you will help keep your intuition clear and sharp. And, conversely, listening to your intuition is a big factor in reducing your stress levels, as it will guide you to avoid stress-producing situations in the first place. Your intuition may also lead you to a stress-management program that's custom-tailored to your interests, schedule, and budget.

Introducing the Four Clairs

We use four senses—*feeling* (which includes taste and smell), *seeing, hearing,* and *thinking*—to connect with the world. When we encounter something new, we automatically check in with ourselves to notice how we feel about this situation. We vigilantly scan for anything dangerous. We listen for unusual sounds, as well as pay attention to our thoughts. (Yes, thinking is also a sense, the one through which we process information.)

These are primal responses we inherited from our ancestors, who had to depend upon their instincts to survive while they foraged for food in the wild. We share these same instincts with all sentient beings.

For example, if it starts to rain, you see, hear, and feel the raindrops, and you process what you think about the change in weather. You can also taste and smell the rain, which falls under the category of feeling. You use these physical senses in response to physical situations.

We have corresponding *inner* senses, which we use to process *energy.* As discussed before, studies show that our limbic, nervous, and endocrine systems can pick up on positive and negative energy before our physical senses are aware of it. This is our intuition instinct. The four inner senses are:

- **Clairsentience,** which means "clear feeling."
- **Clairvoyance,** which means "clear seeing."
- **Clairaudience,** which means "clear hearing."
- **Claircognizance,** which means "clear thinking or knowing."

Since intuition is a normal part of human reasoning and decision-making processes (as the scientific studies show), it seems that the four clairs may operate automatically and unconsciously. The question is whether we notice these responses, and whether we trust their validity. (How many times have you defied a gut feeling, only to later regret not heeding it?)

In other words, you already *are* intuitive, even if you're not consciously aware of your intuitive process. Yet, being aware of your intuition has benefits, including:

- Having more confidence in your decisions
- Trusting the answers you receive intuitively
- Understanding and appreciating yourself

In the following chapters, we'll explore each of these inner senses and look at which foods lead to a heightening of your natural intuitive abilities.

CHAPTER TWO

THE CHAKRAS AND THE FOUR "CLAIRS"

Every one of us has our own intuitive gifts. You don't have to do anything to "attract" your intuition. It's already a vital part of you. In fact, you share a physiological and energetic link with each of your "clairs" via your chakras.

The Chakras

Chakras are energy centers located all over your body that both absorb and send out different vibrations. The word *chakra* means "wheel" in Sanskrit—one of the world's oldest languages—because these energy centers spin around like a wheel, similar to the visual of water swirling down a drain.

Just as light has different-colored wavelengths according to the speed of its vibration, so do the chakra energy wheels appear in an array of colors. For example, in the spectrum, red is one of the slowest vibrations, and purple is one of the fastest. If you were to hook colors up to an oscilloscope (an instrument used to measure the frequency of an electrical signal over time), you would see waves on a graph to indicate their rate of speed. Red would have long, stretched-out waves, while purple would appear as a busy wavy line.

The chakras in the lower part of the body have the slowest vibrations, which correspond to warm-energy colors (red, orange, and yellow). Traveling up the body along the endocrine system, each chakra has a progressively faster-spinning wheel. Therefore, the colors above the waist represent faster-moving, cool colors of green, blue, and purple.

Most people know about the seven major chakras: *crown, third eye, throat, heart, solar plexus, sacral,* and *root.* They run up the center of your body, with two additional important chakras on either side of your head (your *ear* chakras):

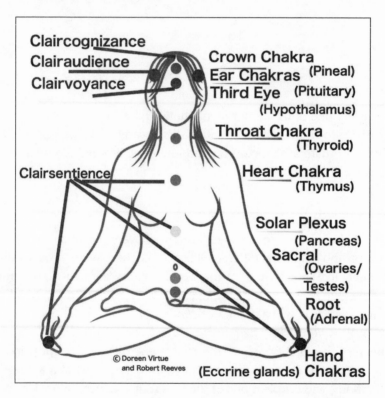

Each chakra is given the job of processing a specific kind of energy. The psychic energy associated with clairsentience is linked to your heart and solar-plexus chakras; clairvoyance to your third-eye chakra; clairaudience to your ear chakras; and claircognizance to your crown chakra.

Chakra	Location	Corresponding Issues	Color
Crown	Inside the top of the head	Claircognizance; Divine guidance	Royal purple
Third eye	Between the eyes	Clairvoyance	Dark blue
Ear	Above the eyebrows	Clairaudience	Violet red
Throat	Adam's apple	Communication; speaking your truth	Light blue
Heart	Center of chest	Clairsentience; love	Emerald green
Solar plexus	Stomach area	Clairsentience; power and control	Yellow
Sacral	3 to 4 inches below the solar plexus	Physical desires and appetites; addictions	Orange
Root	Base of spine	Survival and sustenance concerns, such as money, shelter, and basic material needs	Red

Ancient wisdom and modern psychic studies contend that the body possesses hundreds of these energy centers. In fact, each hand displays its own rainbow of chakra colors throughout the palm and fingers. (As you might expect, the hand chakras are linked to your *feeling* psychic sense—clairsentience.)

When your chakra system is unbalanced, your life can become unbalanced. All your chakras are connected, so when you focus on some of the larger energy centers, the others become cleansed and balanced, too.

By nourishing your various chakras, you can clear the channels of your clairs—and enhance your *feeling, seeing, hearing,* and *knowing* intuition.

Feeling: Clairsentient Intuition

You can receive messages from a combination of the four clairs (clairsentience, clairvoyance, clairaudience, and claircognizance). Usually, though, one of them is your primary way of connecting with the physical and the spiritual world.

The most prevalent form of intuition is *clairsentience,* which involves your physical and emotional feelings. Here are some examples of clairsentience:

- You get a feeling that a certain person is going to call, and he or she does.

- Something in your gut guides your decision, and it turns out to be the correct one.

- You can sense the presence of another person around you, even if you can't see or hear anyone.

- You smell your late grandmother's favorite perfume when none is physically present at that moment (a sign from Heaven).

- You meet someone new and get a bad feeling about the person, which proves to be justified.

Clairsentience, like all forms of intuition, has practical applications. While "being psychic" is associated with alternative lifestyles, the truth is that highly successful people and those who work in dangerous occupations (emergency workers, for instance) all rely upon their gut instincts. Entrepreneurs follow hunches about business prospects, and police officers depend upon their feelings for survival. The intuitive skills inherited from our ancient ancestors serve us well in modern times.

There's scientific evidence for kinesthetic (feeling-based) intuition as well. Studies show that the heart and nervous system respond to a stimulus two to five seconds before it is presented. Listening to the body's signals (such as heart rate, muscle tension, and so forth) will help you to navigate through life.

Likewise, our bodies can also sense the presence of a loved one, even when our conscious minds cannot. Such is the case with a cognitive disorder known as *prosopagnosia,* or "face blindness," as described by social psychologist David G. Myers in this excerpt from the book *Intuition: Its Powers and Perils*:

> Patients with this disorder have suffered damage to a part of the brain involved in face recognition. After losing the pertinent temporal lobe area, patients may have complete sensation but incomplete perception. They can sense visual information—indeed, may accurately report the features of a face yet be unable to recognize it. When shown an unfamiliar face, they do not react. When shown a loved one's face, however, their body displays recognition. Their autonomic nervous system responds with measurable perspiration and speeded pulse. What the conscious mind cannot understand, the heart knows.

In other words, our bodies have the ability to recognize the presence of a loved one through our intuitive senses when our brains are incapable of registering it.

Clairsentience means that your body is attuned to the energy surrounding it and reacts accordingly. High-vibrational energy such as love results in the body relaxing. Low vibrations such as fear or anger result in the body tensing, followed by one of the three types of automatic responses:

- **Fight**—arguing; standing up for yourself; physically defending yourself

- **Flight**—running away physically from the situation; detaching or dissociating

- **Freeze**—"deer in headlights" response, where you feel physically or emotionally helpless and may be temporarily paralyzed with fear

Clairsentience involves the entire body, which feels and responds to vibrations. Thus it is based on several energetic points (namely, the solar-plexus, heart, and hand chakras). Let's go over each one individually here.

Solar-Plexus Chakra

Language is filled with references to the clairsentience/solar-plexus connection. Consider how frequently you hear phrases such as the following:

- *I had a gut feeling about that!*
- *My gut tells me . . .*
- *I can't stomach this situation.*
- *I'm hungry for change.*
- *I feel butterflies in my stomach.*

All these references to the "gut" are really pointing to the solar-plexus chakra, which is located in your navel area. Ancient chakra teachings hold that the solar plexus is the energy center responding to power and control issues. It is hypersensitive to any vibrations in which someone else is trying to overpower or control you.

When you feel the energy of someone who intends to use or abuse you, your stomach muscles tighten in preparation for "fight, flight, or freeze." Happily, the solar-plexus chakra and stomach muscles also respond to trustworthy people by relaxing.

Clairsentient people often pass off their guidance as "just a gut feeling." But if you're clairsentient, your gut feeling is so insistent and so accurate that you need to trust it. Your internal lie detector is turned on 200 percent, so please don't discount those feelings. Listen to your gut when you first meet somebody and when you go to a new location.

Experts believe that we make many of our decisions through a combination of reason and intuition, using our emotional and physical feelings. These intuitive impulses are barely perceived until you resolve to pay attention to your under-the-surface feelings . . . which is a key to becoming increasingly intuitive.

Heart Chakra

The advice "Listen to your heart" is an acknowledgment that this is a center of emotional wisdom. The heart is a truth-teller that gives us guidance that can seem illogical yet usually leads us on a path of happiness and fulfillment.

The ancients envisioned the heart chakra in the center of the chest, glowing bright green. The heart marks the first chakra (going upward from toe to head) that has the faster-moving, cool coloring. Because green is a blend of the yellow from the solar plexus and the blue from the throat chakra, the heart chakra builds a bridge from the lower to the upper body. It's also a bridge between the lower and higher vibrations.

— The heart emits the strongest electromagnetic (EM) fields of any part of the body. In fact, the heart's EM fields are 60 to 100 times stronger than the brain's and can be measured from a distance.

The heart's EM-field rhythms are also influenced by those of other people in the vicinity. Studies have found that when we resonate with others, our heart rates synchronize. Perhaps this is why practitioners of traditional Chinese medicine are taught to calm and center their hearts prior to working with patients.

— The heart has its own "brain." Neurocardiologists have identified that the heart has its own nervous system that learns and processes information, separate from the cortical brain. In some cases, studies have shown that the heart sends signals to the brain, influencing our thinking. This makes sense, as emotions often color our thoughts.

For example, experiments by Dean Radin and researchers at the University of Nevada placed individuals in a doctor's examining room while wearing heart and blood-pressure monitors. In a different room, a researcher asked another person to think either positive or negative thoughts about the person wearing the monitors. The two people didn't know and couldn't see each other. The person wearing the monitors wasn't aware of this experiment.

Whenever the stranger would think positive thoughts about the monitored person, the latter's heart rate and blood pressure would decrease. When negative thoughts were directed toward the person, his or her heart rate and blood pressure increased. *The body literally responds to good and bad vibes.*

— **The heart is psychic.** Heart-response studies have shown that the heart reacts *before* the conscious mind is aware of a stimulus. For example, Rollin McCraty, Ph.D., of the HeartMath Institute conducted an experiment in which 26 people were shown randomly generated "calm" photos (such as landscapes) or "emotional" photos (such as erotic or violent images) while their hearts were monitored. During the experiment, heart-rate-variability responses changed significantly 4.75 seconds before emotional photos were shown. That means that the heart can sense when something emotionally charged is about to happen. It reacts ahead of time, by decreasing or increasing the rate at which it beats.

The study also found that the heart reacts identically to a stimulus whether it's forthcoming or clearly present. In other words, the heart doesn't second-guess its intuitive feelings—it reacts the same, because it trusts what it *knows* is coming next. We can all learn from positive example set by our hearts!

The HeartMath researchers concluded: "The heart is directly involved in the processing of information about a future emotional stimulus, seconds before the body actually experiences the stimulus . . . the heart appears to play a direct role in the perception of future events" (McCraty, Atkinson, and Bradley 2004).

— **The heart is impacted by emotions.** Physicians have long realized that strong human emotions affect our physiology, and now scientific research supports this contention. For instance, it's been shown that people's cardiovascular health *can* suffer due to a broken heart. First identified as *Takotsubo cardiomyopathy* in Japan, this condition is popularly referred to as "broken-heart syndrome" by researchers in the West. The symptoms mimic a heart attack.

According to a Harvard Medical School report, broken-heart syndrome is preceded by life stress, including accidents, weather disasters, sudden surprises, intense fear, receipt of bad news, arguments, financial loss, the death of a loved one, and illness. Then, after suffering a trauma, the person is so distressed that adrenaline and other stress hormones reduce blood flow to the heart, temporarily enlarging part of it. Researchers estimate that 2.5 percent of people seeking heart-attack treatment are actually suffering from broken-heart syndrome.

So our hearts are highly sensitive to stress. If you hold on to hurt, your heart chakra will dim—and, therefore, be less effective in communicating with you. However, if you take the time to heal from past emotional wounds (by journaling, grieving, getting support from a group or a counselor, or another method), then your heart chakra can be healthy and bright . . . and an effective communicator.

Again, modern science is verifying this ancient wisdom. A 2014 study found that depression significantly impairs our intuitive abilities. Just when you are most in need of intuitive guidance to pull yourself out of the blues, it's most difficult to reach. Researchers say that depression makes it challenging for us to focus, which limits our ability to access intuitive information. So, getting help for depression is healthy for your heart, your life . . . and your intuition.

Hand Chakras

As you've read so far, the body knows what's coming its way, reacting with preparations to fight or flee in the face of potential danger. The hands are an important part of the body's sensing tools.

As we mentioned, the seven classic chakras are the most familiar to people, yet the majority of chakras are actually in the hands. Perhaps because the hands have a disproportionately large number of sensory neuronal connections to the nervous system (being our chief sensors and our connectors with the outer world), they also have many chakras.

The hands are extremely energy sensitive and intuitive. For example, physical therapists and massage therapists talk about the "intuitive hand" phenomenon, where their hands act like divining rods magnetically drawn to their clients' areas of soreness. There's a related movement among yoga teachers to gently use intuition to correct student postures with their hands.

The palms exhibit the same "prestimulus" reaction that was described in the heart studies earlier. In an experiment reported in 2003, 125 male and female participants had electrodes taped to their hands, connected to a skin-conductance monitor. A sound—which was either calm or loud and startling—was then randomly generated. Significantly, the participants' palms elicited skin-conductance responses *more than three seconds prior* to the startle sound. The palms knew that something frightening was on the horizon.

A follow-up study in 2005 by other researchers replicated this research. The second study even found, more precisely, that the palms react 3.5 seconds prior to the person hearing a random startle sound.

Our hands seem to have "brains" in them, too! Several decades ago, in an attempt to heal people with serious brain injuries, surgeons would split the connective tissue between the left and the right hemispheres. Much research was conducted on subjects who underwent this surgery, as it resulted in a person with a split consciousness and divided awareness.

One such study showed that hands have a mind of their own, as David G. Myers describes in *Intuition*:

> In an early experiment, psychologist Michael Gazzaniga asked split-brain patients to stare at a dot as he flashed HE•ART. Thus HE appeared in their left visual field (which transmits to the right brain) and ART in the right field (which transmits to the left brain). When he then asked them what they had seen, the patients said they saw ART and so were startled when their left hands (controlled by the right brain) pointed to HE. Given an opportunity to express itself, each hemisphere reported only what it had seen. The left hand intuitively knew what it could not verbally report.
>
> Similarly, when a picture of a spoon was flashed to their right brain, the patients could not say what they saw. But when asked to identify what they had seen by feeling an assortment of hidden objects with their left hands, they readily selected the spoon. If the experimenter said, "Right!" the patient might reply, "What? Right?

How could I possibly pick out the right object when I don't know what I saw?" It is, of course, the left brain doing the talking here, bewildered by what its nonverbal right brain quietly knows.

These experiments demonstrate that the right brain understands simple requests and easily perceives objects. In fact, the right brain is superior to the left at copying drawings, recognizing faces, perceiving differences, sensing and expressing emotion.

Intuitive artists allow their hands free rein to express themselves creatively. The same holds true with champion tennis players and golfers: they trust, let go, and allow their bodies to do what they know how to do.

For personal and healing purposes, I (Doreen) frequently use my hand chakras. For example, I will run my dominant hand (the one favored for writing) an inch or two above someone when I'm giving an in-person session. In this way, I receive a great deal of intuitive information about the person's thought and emotional patterns.

In addition, I've found that we can hold out a hand in the direction of a place we are considering going, and it will give yes-or-no feedback about whether that venture would be productive or a waste of time. This feedback is processed as an inner knowingness.

Seeing: Clairvoyant Intuition

Clairvoyance translates the energies that you feel into visual symbols and messages. There are many forms of clairvoyance, ranging from the rare experience of seeing a full three-dimensional vision with your eyes open to more common clairvoyant experiences such as:

- Having a dream that proves to be prophetic
- Seeing sparkling lights, with no medical cause or physical origin
- Seeing something move out of the corner of your eye, and there's nothing or no one there
- Having visions in your mind's eye

23

Clairvoyance means the ability to clearly see—that is, your psychic sense is visual. You can understand here that the term *clairvoyant* is not necessarily the same as *psychic.* A person who is psychic very well may have clairvoyance but may not use that as his or her primary psychic sense.

Being clairvoyant means that you are highly perceptive with your physical sight and rely on your vision in every aspect of your life. You'll walk into somebody's house and instantly see that the picture frame is crooked. You can close your eyes and recall mental images of yesterday's activities. It also means you could be sensitive to bright lights. You might find it difficult to be out in full daylight without sunglasses or protective eyewear.

With clairvoyance, you receive Divine messages visually. As we mentioned, you may see little sparkles or flashes of light, or something appearing out of the corner of your eye. In the absence of medical issues, seeing sparkling lights is a sign of clairvoyant abilities. What you're observing is the energy exchange between you and your angels.

You'll perceive different colors of light as you become more comfortable with your clairvoyance. White light is generally your personal guardian angels. Bright, vivid cobalt-blue light is a sign that Archangel Michael is with you. Emerald-green sparkles of light indicates that Archangel Raphael is near.

You don't have to behold these visions with your physical eyes. Many times they're in your mind's eye. People often get hung up on the idea that they are meant to see their angels like they do people— as distinct, opaque beings right in front of them. However, you may still be clairvoyant with your eyes closed.

Third-Eye Chakra

The ancients recognized the energy center between the two physical eyes, calling it the *Ajna,* or "brow chakra." Today, we refer to it as the *third-eye chakra,* because it's literally a third eye between your physical eyes. If you meditate upon this area, you will eventually see a mental image of your own third eye. It looks identical to your other two eyes—except there isn't a trace of stress or pain discernible. It's the eye of your Higher Self, which stays above all forms of negativity and looks back at you with pure unconditional love. Energetically, your third eye is housed in a pyramid-shaped membrane that shields it from fear and stress.

Like a movie camera that's always filming, your third eye sees *the energetic truth* about everything you experience. It records everyone's real feelings in a "video" that you can watch periodically, or save for your life review at the end of your mortal time on Earth.

The third eye has the potential to be covered with the energetic equivalent of a camera lens cap. You'll still be recording visual information, but the lens cap will prevent you from seeing it on a daily basis. This occurs when people are afraid of the possibility of clairvoyant visions. Perhaps they fear "losing control" or are worried about seeing a frightening image.

Removing the lens cap requires that you make a conscious decision to see clairvoyantly. I (Doreen) created a nine-video online course to help with this process, called "Clairvoyance Therapy" (available on my EarthAngel.com website). This book also offers guidance for clearing all your chakras, including the third eye.

Hearing: Clairaudient Intuition

With our next psychic sense, we focus upon hearing, called *clairaudience.*

If you are mostly hearing oriented in your life, then your primary clair is likely clairaudience. Sounds are your psychic channel. For example, when you hear songs on the radio or in your mind, you discern that they carry meaningful messages. Chances are, the lyrics are significant for you, or the person you associate with that music is trying to connect with you. Or, upon awakening, you hear your name spoken . . . but no one is there.

When you're clairaudient, you'll hear God and the angels speak directly to you, just as though you're having a conversation with a dear friend. Their voice may be external to your body, so you may hear it as a whispering in your ear; or you may hear it internally, as a voice inside your mind.

You'll know it's not an auditory hallucination, as those are always negative. On the same note, the voice of the ego speaks of elevating you above others or "coaches" you about some get-rich-quick scheme. In a happy contrast, messages from God and the angels are always loving and positive.

In the beginning, that voice may sound similar to your own. The ego has a field day with this! You tell yourself that you're making it up, or that it's just your own thoughts. Yes, you're hearing your own voice, but in spiritual truth, that's the voice that you'll be most comfortable hearing. That's the voice that feels most familiar and the safest. God and the angels come through on that frequency. As you become more and more comfortable, more and more relaxed, they begin to speak to you in different voices and in different ways.

If you are clairaudient, you're also sensitive to sounds. You're often affected by different types of music, and it's likely that you get overwhelmed by noise. So you avoid loud places and prefer quieter music rather than listening at full volume. Since sounds and words are your psychic gift, you probably steer clear of negative talk and harsh language. If you spend time around people who gossip, you may get physical symptoms like headaches.

Honor your sensitivity as the spiritual gift that it is, and adjust your lifestyle toward gentle sounds. For example, play soft music in your home and spend time with people who have pleasant voices, with respectful vocabulary. Buy high-quality earplugs or noise-canceling headphones for those times when you'll encounter loudness. The point is to take control of your auditory environment to give yourself comfort and also to protect your sensitive inner and outer sense of hearing.

Ear Chakras

The energy centers supporting and regulating clairaudience are known as the *ear chakras,* located in between each ear and eyebrow. Reddish violet in color, these energy centers allow you to clearly hear the voice of God, Holy Spirit, your Higher Self, or anyone else whom you hold the intention of hearing.

The ear chakras become blocked with lower energies, primarily from any verbal abuse you've heard from yourself or others. Anytime anyone puts you down—including self-put-downs—the ear chakras absorb this energy like a sponge. They are also affected by hearing negative words and frightening sounds. If the ear chakras aren't cleared of the negative messages, they act like a vacuum cleaner that needs its filter cleaned.

In Part III, you'll read about ways to clear your ear chakras. To maintain their cleanliness, steer clear of negativity in sounds, such as media reports or people who speak harshly. Use loving words as you think or speak of yourself. Gentle and uplifting music and situations are the most supportive.

Knowing: Claircognizant Intuition

Claircognizance is when you receive information as an instant download. You just know, without knowing *how* you know. Claircognizant people are sometimes called know-it-alls, because, quite frankly, they are! They don't have a rational explanation for how they obtained this information, because it's Heaven-sent. They receive Divine guidance through thoughts that just magically pop up.

You're claircognizant if you know who's knocking at the door before you answer it or who's calling you before you've seen the caller ID. So many times claircognizant people will say something like, "Hmm, we haven't seen Aunt Mary for a while, have we?" Then that day she appears at your doorstep.

Some examples of claircognizance include:

- Knowing how to do something complicated, without receiving prior instruction.

- Meeting someone new and having an instant knowingness (information, not feelings) about that person.

- Having knowledge come pouring through you when you speak or write . . . and you didn't know those facts before

- Receiving million-dollar ideas (even if you don't follow through on them)

The scientific annals are filled with research about claircognizance. One of the leading researchers on the topic, John Bargh, describes it as *automatic unconscious knowing.* And Princeton University psychologist Daniel Kahneman notes, "Intuitive thinking is perception-like, rapid, effortless." By contrast, "deliberate thinking is reasoning-like, critical, and analytic" (Myers 2002).

In other words, claircognizants receive their information internally. If this sounds like you, the key is learning to trust your knowingness. Logically, you (or others) may question *how* you know what you know. Trust the intuitive process, which is similar to having a download of information suddenly appear in your mind.

If you're claircognizant, you need to pay very close attention to your thoughts . . . and please share them with others. So many times in our travels we've met claircognizant people who don't voice the wisdom that they receive, because they assume it's common knowledge. Understand that the wisdom you have as a matter of course may be profoundly and spiritually life-changing for everybody else.

Crown Chakra

The *crown chakra* crowns the chakras within our bodies. It is essential to receiving thoughts, information, and ideas from the Divine mind or collective unconscious. Those who are highly claircognizant can tap into the wealth of creativity and inventions that abound in the spiritual plane. A clean crown chakra glows in a beautiful, rich shade of purple, interspersed with sparkles of diamond-white light. Crown chakras clogged with unhealed emotions and bitter thoughts about Divine guidance, God, or negative religious experiences look as dark as the night sky. Fortunately, the chakras respond quickly to nutrient-rich, cleansing foods and clearing techniques such as detox-ing (described in Part II and Part III).

Asking for the Information to Be Clearer

Your intuition is the way you receive Divine messages. So it's important that they come through clearly! Throughout this book we will share nutritional methods and techniques that will enhance your natural abilities. To complement this, we also recommend asking for clearer information.

If you were chatting with someone and the person was talking too softly, you would ask him or her to please speak up. You can do the very same with your intuitive guidance! If you hear a message but it's too quiet, ask for it to come through louder. If you see a rapid vision in your mind, ask to see the image again but more slowly.

Many people forget, or don't even realize, that they can request that their intuitive messages be clearer and more comfortable for them.

Your Primary Clair

Now that we've looked at the four types of intuition—clairsen-tience, clairvoyance, clairaudience, and claircognizance—you may be wondering which applies to you. Everyone has the capacity for each of these psychic senses, as they are part of our physiology. That is to say, we all have clairvoyance, we all have clairaudience, we all have clairsentience, and we all have claircognizance. It's usual, though, that one or two of them are stronger and perhaps more developed than the others, and this is how your intuition "speaks" to you the loudest.

Your *primary clair* is the main way in which you notice the outside world and the inner world of intuition, and corresponds with one of the following sensory orientations:

— **Kinesthetic (clairsentient).** This means that you connect to the world through your physical and emotional feelings. You moni-tor how you feel in situations and relationships to determine your next step. When you meet someone, you notice how you feel in his or her presence to ascertain whether you want to spend more time with him or her or not. You can sense when something is right or "off." You use emotions to make decisions, and you tend to follow your heart. You are extremely sensitive to energy and can pick up on others' emotions. In fact, if you're not careful, you take on other people's problems as if they were your own. Extremely compassionate and empathetic, you are also aware of your physical feelings. You notice how your body reacts, and you trust these messages. You also have a keen sense of smell and taste.

— **Visual (clairvoyant).** Your eyes are your connection to the world, and you notice and appreciate beauty. You have a photographic memory and learn best by seeing processes demonstrated. You don't like pictures on the wall to be crooked, and you prefer visual balance and order. You have vivid dreams, even if you can't remember them. You watch what people do, rather than what they say, to determine their integrity. Many of your intuitive messages are received as visuals in your mind's eye. You may see a vision of a symbol, a flash of an image, or even a mental movie. You may also see sparkling or flashing lights, and your eyes and body are perfectly healthy.

— **Auditory (clairaudient).** You relate to the world through the sounds you hear. You pay attention to the melody and inflexion of someone's voice more than you do to his or her words. You hear songs in your mind as a primary way of receiving Divine messages. You may have also heard celestial music or your name being called without any physical presence to account for these sounds. You may hear a high-pitched ringing sound in one ear, with no medical origins (this is the sound of Heaven trying to get your attention). You could receive "Divine dictation" from God's voice, if you choose to: Simply go to a writing platform like a computer or sit at your desk with a pen and paper, and begin to ask questions aloud or silently. Then type or write the answers you hear. The truth always "clicks" with you.

— **Cognitive (claircognizant).** You process everything through your thoughts, noticing whether it makes sense or you can learn something from it. Knowledge is your priority, and you love to learn.

You have a sense of knowingness, where you know things without any logical explanation for "how" you know. If someone asks you a question, you'll deliver the answer as if you're channeling an encyclopedia. For this reason, you may have been teased as a know-it-all. You are able to fix things without looking at instructions. You receive great ideas for inventions. However, you may talk yourself out of pursuing them because you're certain that everyone knows what you know. You think your knowledge is common information, but it's not.

To discover which clair is your strongest, pay attention to what you notice when you meet someone new. Are you focused on your feelings (clairsentience); looking at the person's eyes, clothing, hair, and so on (clairvoyance); noticing the sound of his or her voice (clairaudience); or ascertaining whether you think the person is interesting (claircognizance)? The way you process experiences in the physical world is exactly the way you receive Divine guidance.

You can also ask God and the angels a question and pay attention to what comes up:

- If you're *clairsentient,* notice how you feel as you go through your day. When you feel light and happy, it shows you are going in the right direction. If there's some disquiet, look for other ways to approach the situation.

- If you're *clairvoyant,* notice the things that are catching your eye. For instance, why do you keep seeing that store's name? Maybe you need to go there today.

- If you're *clairaudient,* notice what you hear. Do you catch part of a conversation between people sitting behind you? It may be a message for *you.*

- If you're *claircognizant,* notice what you think about today. Did you receive any inspired ideas?

Pay attention to all those sensory experiences and allow your intuition to develop fully in order to embrace it in new and exciting ways. When you eat healthy, natural foods, your intuitive gifts will strengthen. Instead of trying to decipher confusing messages, you'll receive insights that are clear and easy to understand. You'll first notice that your primary clair becomes more accurate and reliable. Then, by continuing to enjoy nutritious foods, you will strengthen your secondary clairs, adding even more detail to the messages and guidance you receive.

In the next chapter we will introduce you to the healing life force of food and how that plays a role in your clairvoyance, clairsentience, clairaudience, and claircognizance.

CHAPTER THREE

CONNECTING TO THE ENERGY OF FOOD

Everything you eat is influencing your body not only physically but also energetically. The energy of different foods, as we'll share with you throughout this book, has a tremendous impact on how you perceive the day and access your intuition.

Your body is your main physical tool for working on your life purpose—the vehicle in which you're able to complete your spiritual journey. Therefore, part of your Divine mission is to take excellent care of yourself. A car needs quality fuel. Similarly, your physical self requires healthy, nutritious, natural foods for long-lasting vitality.

If we flood our system with poor-quality materials, then we're only going to get poor results. The angels have taught us, and you'll discover for yourself, that high-energy foods yield high-energy results.

The simple truth is that you're only issued one body for the entire duration of this lifetime on Earth. That means you'll want to lovingly attend to your physical well-being. You need to be operating at 100 percent so that you can achieve all your dreams. Just like an automobile, your body requires proper maintenance.

Nutrition, then, is the nourishment that your body needs to thrive—not just survive. You don't want a body that just goes through the motions of life. Instead, you want one that's filled with enthusiasm, motivation, and inspiration. So aim for uplifting, high-energy, fresh, easily digestible organic foods and beverages.

Everything you consume, whether food or drink, has a direct influence on your chakra system. With a diet that's high in fats, carbohydrates, and processed foods, your outlook on life can become depleted and miserable. Constantly struggling to get on top of things, you see the world as a harsh environment, where nothing seems to work in your favor.

Conversely, if you change your diet to incorporate more high-energy fruits and vegetables, you'll find that a cloud is lifted. You'll start to feel more positive, with a brighter outlook on what's to come. You'll be more confident and motivated to take action on behalf of your spiritual purpose.

For example, tropical fruits are amazing not just for their flavor, but also for their high energy and vibration. Think about how these foods grow, sitting outside in the warm sunlight all day long. They're soaking in that high-energy, uplifting, powerful vibration from the sun. They transform the solar energy into valuable nutrition for you, and as you consume that wonderful mango, pineapple, or papaya, your body is absorbing that vibration. In a sense, it's an edible form of sunshine.

What happens, we have seen clairvoyantly, is that the energy of the sun goes through that food and into your body. It then spreads out to nourish every single one of your body's chakras. It illuminates them with that light from above. You begin to shine from within. Each of your cells is reinvigorated as it captures the essence of motivation.

Simply by changing your diet, you can change your outlook on life. Similarly, we are going to show you how you can nutritionally switch on your very natural psychic abilities. Your intuition is already a part of who you are; it just needs the cloud to be lifted.

Your Endocrine System and Chakras

We have high respect for ancient healing systems, including the time-honored Eastern traditions of Ayurveda. Our ancestors lived in sync with nature and therefore reaped the benefit of having their intuition and clairvoyance fully awakened. These ancient healers provided us with road maps of the human energy systems—the chakras—well before medicine had magnetic-resonance scanning to acknowledge that the human body uses electrical impulses.

Prior to the advent of these imaging tools, many scientists scoffed at the idea of electric charges in the body. Now, it's confirmed that the brain/nervous system "speaks" to itself via synapses carrying energy.

The ancients could see these energy fields within the body. They noticed that the energy is particularly strong around the endocrine glands, a system that manages our connection with the outside world. As mentioned earlier, the endocrine system—including the hypothalamus, adrenals, and pituitary—help us respond to stressful situations and later to recover from stress.

Each chakra has a corresponding endocrine gland (and vice versa). Here is a diagram outlining the correspondence:

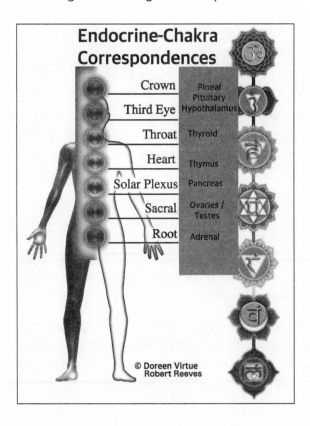

In addition, the chakras and endocrine glands provide you with biofeedback according to how you process information about the world. For example, if meeting new people is stressful for you, your chakras will close and darken to protect you, and your endocrine glands will pour stress hormones into your system. However, if you enjoy making new friends, your chakras will brighten and enlarge, and your endocrine glands won't have to work so hard. So how your chakras and endocrine glands react is not cut-and-dried.

Sometimes our bodies can sense when someone or something carries negative intentions. Our ancient cave-person brain processes this energy as the equivalent of danger, and sends warning signals through our chakras and endocrine glands. Yet, other times, it's our *beliefs* about a situation—not the actual situation—which cause stress responses in the body.

Regardless, the chakras and endocrine glands are sensors of energies. They are your feelers that guide and warn you as you navigate through the world. They alert you to danger and escort you to positive situations.

The Endocrine System as Portal to Your Clairs

Each endocrine gland associated with your chakras corresponds to a different aspect of intuition—that is, one of your inner senses: clairsentience, clairvoyance, clairaudience, and claircognizance.

Clairsentience

Clairsentience is affected by the endocrine glands located in our feeling centers: the solar plexus and heart. In addition, *exocrine* glands can be found in our external feeling centers: the hands. (Exocrine glands act on an outer surface of the body, while endocrine glands work via the bloodstream.)

— The endocrine gland nearest to the solar plexus is the **pancreas.** Located behind the stomach, the pancreas is both an endocrine and an exocrine, busily fulfilling many roles, which include creating and secreting digestive enzymes and producing insulin and glucagon to regulate blood glucose. These substances are involved in digestion and also in the regulation of fear emotions. In a dangerous situation, you need more blood sugar for the energy to fight or flee. The regulation of potentially stressful situations is one of the connections of the pancreas to the solar plexus.

In traditional Chinese medicine, being a happy and positive person is a key to pancreatic health, as is lifelong learning, since the pancreas is connected to the intellect. Practitioners of Chinese medicine say that perfectionism and emotional isolation can contribute to pancreatic health challenges. The pancreas is negatively affected by worrying (the fear of losing power) and perfectionism (the fear of losing control), both traits related to the solar plexus. Similar to Ayurvedic beliefs, Chinese medicine links the stomach, the spleen, and the pancreas to the Earth element, which gives us strength.

Spiritual and energetic healers say that the pancreas is affected by whether you consider life to have "sweetness" or not. Since it is involved in blood-sugar regulation, this makes sense. Feeling a lack of life sweetness can create problems in this area. Louise Hay, the author of *Heal Your Body* and founder of our publisher, Hay House, says that pancreatic issues are triggered by a craving to be loved.

The pancreas/sweetness connection applies in the physical sense also: imbalances in the pancreas can lead to cravings for sugar. Yet, refined sugar is one of the worst substances for your pancreas. Several studies have actually correlated a sugary diet with a statistically higher probability of developing pancreatic cancer. High-fat animal proteins, too, are associated with this type of cancer. Researchers have found that a high-fiber, plant-based diet significantly *lowers* the risk for pancreatic cancer.

When you feed your pancreas the nutrients it *needs,* not what it craves (sugar), you support your own health. These foods nourish your solar plexus, as well, and tend to increase self-confidence so you don't worry so much about control issues. A healthy solar plexus also means that you'll be safer and more successful, because you'll trust your gut feelings.

— The **adrenal glands** sit atop the kidneys, where they produce hormones in response to stress, such as adrenaline, norepinephrine, and hydrocortisone. They also produce aldosterone, a hormone involved in balancing blood pressure and saltwater levels.

Because the adrenals are our first responders to stress, they are associated with the root, or base, chakra, at the bottom of the spine, as well as the sacral chakra, near the stomach. Our diet can support our adrenals—and root and sacral chakras—as follows:

- **First,** it's important to eat at regular intervals. Fasting or skipping meals can tax the adrenals, causing them to work harder to balance the blood sugar by producing more cortisol.

- **Second,** when we're stressed or experiencing low blood sugar, we may crave refined sugar or caffeine to quickly boost our energy. Unfortunately, sugar and caffeine artificially stimulate the adrenals and other glands and organs. We'll get the temporary high, followed by an energy crash.

Our adrenals function best with a balanced whole-grain, organic vegetable-and-fruit diet combined with stress reduction. Studies show that practicing gentle or restorative yoga 35 minutes a day can reduce the amount of cortisol that your adrenals produce. This also promotes healthy weight loss (Virtue 2015)!

— The **thymus** is the endocrine gland associated with the heart chakra. Located in the upper chest, the thymus is the immune-system regulator, directing white blood cells and antibodies. Just like the heart, the thymus is extremely sensitive to negative emotions. When you're under stress, your thymus is working overtime to protect your immune system. Too much chronic stress, though, can trigger illness in this gland.

Your heart *and* thymus work better with a healthful and balanced lifestyle. A clean diet, free of chemicals and other toxins, fuels them both. Getting plenty of exercise and rest is also a prescription for heart and thymus health. The more you can de-stress your life, the happier they are!

Many studies have found that electromagnetic frequencies (EMFs) are harmful to the thymus's cells. Your thymus and heart do better if you:

- Make sure your home is away from electric power lines.

- Don't place electronics (television, radio, electric clock, and so forth) near your bed

- Sit far from the television

- Only use low-EMF appliances and computers

- Monitor your environment with an EMF detector (available for purchase online)

- Unplug your wireless router when not in use and while you sleep

Studies on rats and calves found that taking a melatonin supplement provided significant protection of the thymus from the harmful effects of microwave radiation. (The rat dosage was 2 mg melatonin per kg body weight, but of course check with your own health-care professional to see what's right for you.)

— The hands' intuitive response channels are a combination of the sensory neuronal connections to the nervous system and the **eccrine** sweat glands. After all, your palms perspire when you're anxious, and this holds true when your body is alerting you to something that's about to happen. The skin-conductance-response studies that involved a startling sound exemplify how the eccrine glands are intuitive.

Sweating may also be a response to the foods you eat. This type of perspiration is called *gustatory sweating,* and can be provoked by:

- Spicy foods

- Caffeinated drinks, including soda, coffee, and tea

- Alcoholic beverages

This is different from sweating as a warning sign from your intuition. For that reason, part of the aim of *Nutrition for Intuition* is to guide you to reduce or avoid foods that could trigger "false alarms." If you find that you perspire profusely, you may want to cut down on your intake of these substances.

Clairvoyance, Clairaudience, and Claircognizance

The three clairs located within our heads—clairvoyance, clairaudience, and claircognizance—are also regulated by three members of the endocrine system in the head. Here is a brief overview of each and how it relates to your intuition:

— The **pineal gland** is shaped like a pinecone or pineapple, and in ancient times it was likened to an antenna that received important sensory input. Our ancestors were indeed wise, because there *is* truth to this analogy. The pineal gland regulates visual, auditory, and intuitive thought processes. Physically, the pineal gland produces melatonin, which affects our sleep cycles and light sensitivity. The pineal gland sits next to the third-eye chakra, or *Ajna,* between your two physical eyes, which receives incoming clairvoyant visions.

— Located at the base of the brain, the **pituitary gland** performs several duties, including regulation of body and sexual development and other endocrine glands; production of melanin (skin pigmentation); and production of an antidiuretic hormone to prevent dehydration. In addition, the pituitary gland produces the hormone *oxytocin,* which regulates labor contractions, breast-feeding, and emotional bonding with other people. This "master gland" of the endocrine system also controls the thyroid. The pituitary gland, in turn, is overseen by the hypothalamus.

— The **hypothalamus** is the superpowered regulatory center in the brain that keeps us in balance, in a process called *homeostasis.* It's involved with digestion, body temperature, blood pressure, and fluid balance. In addition, the hypothalamus regulates our appetite, thirst, mood, and sex drive. Also involved with our emotions, it's keeping score of our true feelings at all times.

How Nutrition Affects Your Endocrine System

To fuel its important functions, the endocrine system relies upon nutrients. Here are some key ones for your intuition as well as your overall physical health:

— **Vitamin A,** or *carotene* (found in green leafy, orange, and yellow vegetables such as spinach, carrots, and bell peppers), is involved in immune function, vision, reproduction, and cellular communication.

— **B vitamins:**

- B_1 (found in seeds, beans, peas, and whole grains) is used by the body to metabolize food for energy and to maintain proper heart and nerve function.

- B_5 (found in broccoli, fish, shellfish, chicken, milk, yogurt, legumes, mushrooms, avocado, sweet potatoes, and whole grains) is required for chemical reactions that generate energy from food synthesis of the hormone melatonin.

- B_6 (found in poultry, fish, and organ meats; potatoes and other starchy vegetables; and fruit other than citrus) boosts melatonin and is involved in metabolism, brain development during pregnancy and infancy, and immune function.

- B_{12} (found in fish, fortified cereals, plant-based milks, and fortified yeast extract) helps keep the body's nerve and blood cells healthy. (Vegans must take a supplement for B_{12}, as there are no plant-based sources that are sufficient.)

— **Vitamin C** (found in citrus fruits such as oranges and grapefruit and their juices, as well as red and green peppers, kiwi, broccoli, strawberries, potatoes, and tomatoes) acts as an antioxidant, protecting cells from damage. In addition, vitamin C improves the absorption of iron from plant-based foods and helps the immune system work properly.

— **Vitamin D** (found in fatty fish such as salmon, tuna, and mackerel; fish liver oils; and some mushrooms) promotes calcium absorption in the gut and is needed for other roles in the body, including modulation of cell growth, neuromuscular and immune function, and reduction of inflammation.

— **Iodine** (found in seafood and sea vegetables, cranberries, yogurt, navy beans, strawberries, and potatoes) helps your thyroid respond properly to signals sent from the pituitary gland.

— **Omega-3 fatty acids** (found in salmon, tuna, flaxseeds, flaxseed oil, chia seeds, sardines, nuts, and clove spice) are important for a number of bodily functions, including muscle activity, blood clotting, digestion, fertility, and cell division and growth.

— **Selenium** (found in seafood and meats, cereals and other grains, dairy products, and Brazil nuts) plays critical roles in reproduction, thyroid-hormone metabolism, DNA synthesis, and protection from oxidative damage and infection.

(*A note about phytoestrogens:* These plant-based estrogen-like substances, found in soy products, beans, meat, flax, legumes, tempeh, sesame, and rice, bind to the body's estrogen receptors and can act just like estrogen in the body. The body creates a harmonious balance of hormones, and by overconsuming phytoestrogen-containing foods, you can disturb this balance and disrupt your endocrine system. Aim to rotate the foods you eat.

Studies show that apart from soy products, all phytoestrogens are safe for men and women, with the exception of those who are allergic to these foods. Women who have a family or personal history of breast-health issues are usually counseled to avoid soy products because of their estrogen content. Everyone should avoid genetically modified soy, since a recent study confirmed that soy contains carcinogenic formaldehyde unless it is certified organic and non-genetically modified [Ayyadurai and Deonikar 2015].)

The common denominator of these nutrients is that they support various hormones needed to help the body cope with different events and stresses. The endocrine system works with the nervous system, and is responsible for the secretion of hormones via glands located throughout the body. These hormones help protect us physically and regulate our physiological functions, including heart rate, digestion, metabolism, and more.

Below are nutritional recommendations to keep your your clairs and chakras healthy and balanced, as noted by scientists and nutritionists who have studied the relationship between diet and endocrine health.

Nutrition for Clairsentience

For the **solar-plexus chakra,** nutrition for intuition helps you to:

- Increase self-confidence.
- Lessen control issues.
- Reduce worrying.
- Minimize perfectionism.

For the **heart chakra,** nutrition for intuition helps you to:

- Have clarity about your desires.
- Feel love toward yourself and life.
- Attract other loving people.

For the **hand chakras,** nutrition for intuition helps you to:

- Maintain the health and strength of your hands. (Like other extremities, the hands are subject to cramping or feeling cold without adequate nutrients.)

- Heighten your hands' sensitivity in terms of discerning messages, information, and guidance.

To Nourish Your Solar-Plexus Chakra
(and Adrenals and Pancreas) . . .

Consume:

- Beans and legumes
- Fruit, particularly citrus
- Sea vegetables

Avoid:

- Animal fats
- Fried foods
- Refined sugar
- Alcohol
- Nicotine and cigarettes

To Nourish Your Heart Chakra
(and Thymus) . . .

Consume:

- Cruciferous organic vegetables (broccoli, cauliflower, cabbage)
- Nuts high in vitamin E and omega-3s (walnuts)
- Carotene-rich foods (squash, carrots, yams, sweet potatoes, red peppers, tomatoes, dark greens)
- Vitamin B_6–rich foods (sunflower seeds, pistachios, tuna, bananas, avocados, spinach, beans, lentils, asparagus, broccoli, tropical fruits, oranges)
- Citrus for vitamin C

Avoid:

- Saturated fats
- Cigarettes
- Chemicals
- Refined sugar

To Nourish Your Hand Chakras
(and Eccrines) . . .

Consume:

- Foods high in B vitamins (dark green leafy vegetables, almonds, lentils, fish, bananas, egg yolk, yogurt, avocado)
- Iron-rich foods (beans, fish, meat, spinach, seeds, lentils)
- Magnesium-plentiful foods (dark green leafy vegetables, nuts, seeds, fish, beans, lentils, brown rice, avocado, low-fat organic dairy, bananas)
- Niacin-rich foods (mushrooms, asparagus, corn, fish, meat, nuts, brown rice)
- Foods high in vitamin C (tropical fruit, dark green leafy vegetables, kiwi, broccoli, berries, citrus)

Avoid:

- Foods containing lectin (uncooked legumes such as beans and pulses—well cooked is fine)
- Nightshade-family foods (tomatoes, eggplant, peppers, potatoes)
- Caffeine
- Foods with chemical additives or genetic modification (GMOs)
- Dairy products

- Alcohol
- Refined sugar

Nutrition for Clairvoyance

For the **third-eye chakra,** nutrition for intuition helps you to:

- Enjoy balanced sleep cycles.
- Preserve your physical, as well as your spiritual, sight.

To Nourish Your Third-Eye Chakra
(and Pineal Gland, Pituitary Gland, and Hypothalamus) . . .

Consume:

- Sun-ripened fruits (ripened while still on the tree)—
  pineapple, in particular
- Dark leafy greens

Avoid:

- Caffeine
- Alcohol
- Fluoride (because it calcifies the pineal gland)

Nutrition for Clairaudience

For the **ear chakras,** nutrition for intuition helps you to:

- Preserve your physical, as well as your spiritual, hearing
  abilities.[*]

---

[*] The National Health Examination and Nutrition Survey studied approximately 2,500 people to find a link between diet and the development of hearing loss. They found that those who ate the healthiest (vegetables, fruit, whole grains, and other whole foods) had significantly better hearing, especially at high frequencies, compared to those who ate a junk food or a processed (unnatural) diet.

To Nourish Your Ear Chakras
(and Pineal Gland, Pituitary Gland, and Hypothalamus) . . .

Consume:

- Omega-3-rich foods (wild-caught salmon, trout, sardines, flaxseeds or flaxseed oil, nuts, broccoli)
- Folic acid–containing foods (green leafy vegetables, asparagus, broccoli, citrus fruits, beans, peas, lentils, avocados, Brussels sprouts, seeds, nuts, celery, carrots, squash, corn, cauliflower, rice)
- Magnesium-rich foods (broccoli, bananas, potatoes)

Avoid:

- Fried foods
- Cigarette smoke
- Loud noises

Nutrition for Claircognizance

For the **crown chakra,** nutrition for intuition helps you to:

- Focus and concentrate.
- Prevent "brain fog," where you aren't aware of your own thoughts. (You'll want to avoid foods triggering allergic reactions, as that can lead to brain fog. It's a good idea to get a blood test for dietary allergies and sensitivities so you can steer clear of allergens.)

To Nourish Your Crown Chakra
(and Pineal Gland, Pituitary Gland, and Hypothalamus) . . .

Consume:

- Breakfast each morning, for better cognitive performance

- Omega-3-rich foods (fish, walnuts, pumpkin seeds, flaxseeds)
- Cruciferous vegetables (cabbage, broccoli, cauliflower)
- Flavonoid-containing foods (blueberries, kidney beans)

Avoid:

- Caffeine
- Refined sugar
- Alcohol
- Gluten

The Vibration of Food

Every food has its own individual vibration. When you're in the grocery store, you intuitively pick up on that energy. Consider the process when you'd like to buy some apples. What you naturally do is scan over the assortment on display, choose one in particular, and pop that in your basket. Then you scan again and choose another very specific apple. You don't just go and blindly grab those fruits closest to you.

On an intuitive level, our souls know the perfect foods for us and which ones are going to resonate with our lifestyle. However, if we've become conditioned to eat processed foods, sweeteners, colorings, and added sugars, then these artificial creations may trick us into thinking that we feel satisfied. In truth, these foods are giving us nothing at all. They are just taking up space that valuable high-energy, high-vibrational foods are meant to be occupying.

As you enjoy natural, high-energy foods, the way you look out at and perceive the world is different. You'll no longer buy into a "lack" mentality. You won't heed the doom-and-gloom scenarios, and you won't listen to fear-based stories in the media. Instead, what you'll learn to do is *pray* about those situations. See this as an opportunity to use your knowledge and intentions to help foster peace and balance. You are able to see things in a different light because that light is now coming from *within* you.

If you're consuming healthy, natural foods, you feel positive and uplifted. If, on the other hand, you're consuming heavy, unhealthy foods, then your outlook on life becomes dull and depressed. People often notice that every time they eat a particular food, they immediately feel a certain way physically. However, they may not realize how it changes their emotions, thought processes, and intuition.

We have found so many people who can't see how their energy is affected by what they put in their mouths. They may eat fast food during the evening and then the next morning wake up feeling sluggish and headachy—yet to them, these are two entirely unrelated events. They've made no connection between the food they've eaten and how they feel the next day. We must always remind ourselves that our bodies are very sensitive vessels.

We've seen spiritual professionals—healers and psychic readers—continue to eat in an unhealthy way. We gently explained to them that they might find their abilities enhanced if they chose to eat more intuitively and naturally.

At first these people argued that they didn't need to change their eating habits, because the messages they were receiving were already very strong. And we didn't disagree. We could see that the work they were doing was powerful and certainly healing. Yet the messages our angels were giving us was that those people could achieve even more transformative conversations if they changed some of the foods they were consuming.

We kindly suggested this idea—not putting any pressure on them but rather simply laying the proverbial tools out on the table and asking them to give them a try. On a subconscious level they must have been receiving similar messages, and they willingly followed our recommendations. What they found was that efficacy of the healings they administered and accuracy of the readings they gave skyrocketed! They achieved a level that they didn't even know they could reach, simply by changing a handful of things in their diets.

Now you can understand that what you eat—your nutrition—has a direct impact on how you feel, the subtle signs you receive, and how you perceive the world—your intuition. These two things are Divinely connected and influence one another accordingly.

PART II

Recipes and Recommendations to Nourish Your Intuition

CHAPTER FOUR

GUIDING DIETARY PRINCIPLES

There's no one correct diet for every single person. We have to recognize that we are all individuals and, therefore, our diets need to be right for *us*.

Lifestyle magazines so often feature celebrity diet tips, telling us calorie by calorie what our favorite stars eat during the day. We'll see their breakfast, lunch, and dinner menus, as well as any included snacks. You may have even tried these diets in the past, to no avail.

These eating plans work for *their* individual bodies but may be incompatible with your own. Their energy, their metabolism, and the physical demands on them may be radically different from *your* makeup and lifestyle.

Please don't feel like you've failed if you couldn't stick to those diets. The food *you* need to consume is unique to you. We ask you to try different things, to experiment, and, above all, to trust your own intuition and guidance.

Many individuals experience an increase in their energy and in their spiritual gifts by letting go of animal products. Sometimes, though, people listen to the ego voice, which says that becoming vegetarian is too restrictive and they won't have any food options.

I (Robert) was supporting a patient who felt guided to become vegetarian. We came up with alternatives for lunch and dinner that he felt confident about. He was feeling very positive about the change and explained that this choice was something he had been thinking about making for a while. Then a look of horror crossed his face. "But what will I be able to have for *breakfast?!*" he asked.

I reflected the question back to him, inquiring, "What do you normally have for breakfast?"

He paused for a moment, and then came to the realization that he *never* ate animal protein for breakfast! He could carry on enjoying his muesli while he was moving toward vegetarianism.

I think this is such a powerful reminder of how we can often be conditioned to think that giving up meat is a challenge. It may very well be easier than we suspect.

Similarly, your ego might say that being vegan is going to make it too hard to connect with friends and family over lunches or dinners. Please don't dismiss these ways of eating before you've experienced them for yourself.

Rather than throwing those ideas out the window, try them for a bit and see how they make you feel. If you feel better, you form a stronger connection to God and your angels, your intuition increases, and you start to have a spring in your step and renewed joy in life, then that's a clear sign that eating this way is beneficial for you.

Honor Your Uniqueness

Eating healthy looks different for everyone, because each body is created in a unique, special way. Your dietary requirements are unlike those of anybody else who's currently living. Some may demand higher amounts of protein. Others might need more complex carbohydrates to keep their energy levels high. There's no right or wrong answer when it comes to the foods you choose, so focus on the energy they contain. Is the food "alive" as you consume it? Are you taking in positive and uplifting vibrations? Or is that food basically lifeless? If there's no life force, it isn't going to bring *you* any vitality and, frankly, is just a whole heap of useless calories.

Trust your intuition when it comes to food choices, as your Higher Self will always tell you the truth. If you pick up a candy bar and hear or feel God and the angels say, *This isn't going to do you any good,* trust that message. Listen to what they say because they have your best interests at heart.

The way we prepare food is an individual process, too. Some people do very well on a raw diet comprising mostly fruits and vegetables. Others prefer lightly steaming veggies, while still others enjoy stir-frying them with healthy seasonings like tamari or almond butter. All these options are correct and healthy! We would never say that everybody should have only raw food . . . or steam everything they eat.

Instead, we want to give you tools so you can do your own personal experiments. Try a different way of eating for a week or two and gauge the result. Has your intuition become more accurate? If it has, then maintain that way of eating. If you feel dull or less energetic, something's gone wrong. These are signs that you're not getting everything you need from the food you're eating.

The truth is, there's no "perfect" way to eat that suits everyone. Yet, with our many years of personal experience, and the testimony of the thousands of workshop participants we have spoken to, we've found common threads that appear to work for most people.

Thoughts on the Paleo Diet: Ancient Dietary Concepts

There are some things about the Paleo diet that we really like . . . and others that we find really challenging, as sensitive people and as vegetarians and vegans. The Paleo diet is modeled on the Paleolithic era, when early humans ate only foods that they could either hunt or gather. The theory behind this way of eating is that we have evolved very little genetically over the last few thousand years. However, in that same time frame, agricultural development has advanced by leaps and bounds.

We now mass-produce grains, cereals, and legumes, which were never a part of our ancestors' diets. These are new foods, from the perspective of our genetic makeup. Theories suggest that when we eat grains—like wheat, rye, barley, and oats—or lentils and beans, our bodies do not know how to break them down. This may lead to small amounts of inflammation arising in the body. Inflammation of any kind causes stress to our system, and whether of short- or long-term duration, it may lead to other health concerns.

We wondered: Is it because, evolutionarily, the body is unable to keep up with our dietary changes . . . or is it just that we're overdoing that particular food group?

If you look at the diet of the general population these days, it is mostly made up of grains. The next item that's overconsumed is meat. For the average person, every meal is usually going to contain meat products and gluten.

We asked the angels if this is something that we needed to be more conscious of. The angels said yes, but not necessarily because it's too much for our genetics to handle. Instead, they reminded us that *any* food we eat in excess is going to become an issue. Even healthy items like green leafy vegetables can be problematic if they're the only things you enjoy. If you sit down and eat a bowl of kale for breakfast, lunch, and dinner every day of the week, sooner or later your body is going to start to resist it.

Well, we like to test things out on ourselves, and what we found is that when we cut back on grains, we *did* feel better. Our weight loss increased even when we didn't attempt to be conscious of calories. The pounds we shed weren't unhealthy muscle loss, either, but rather the release of mild inflammation and excess fluid. You'd be amazed by how much fluid grains attract!

If you follow a vegetarian or a vegan lifestyle, then the Paleo diet can be very tough to adhere to. As a naturopath, I (Robert) have many clients come see me and say they're on the latest and greatest diet. So, when some initially talked about the Paleo diet, I instantly started researching and reading up on it. It's heavily into animal prod- ucts, and as someone who enjoys vegetarian food, I found it difficult to even try eating this particular way. I like lots of protein, and I know we can get it from plant sources. But one of the diet plans I was look- ing at suggested that I personally should be eating around 36 eggs in a single week. I felt this was *way* too many.

That being said, this isn't the entire premise that the Paleo diet is based on. You don't *have* to sit down and eat meat and eggs as your only protein sources. You can follow Paleo as a vegetarian, or even as a vegan, but it just takes more planning.

In the Paleo way of eating, we're also advised to avoid all dairy products. No other species on the planet drinks the milk from a different species. Therefore, our bodies may have a difficult time processing milk intended for baby cows, goats, or even sheep. It's completely foreign to us. It makes sense that our genetic makeup might not be ready to break down and digest the protein and vitamins contained in a food designed for a species we aren't even closely related to.

The Paleo diet is strict, and as we've stated, there are some things that resonate with us and others that don't. What we'd like you to take away from this style of eating is its encouragement of good amounts of protein. When you eat adequate protein, your body (and brain) has the fuel it needs to achieve amazing things.

We recommend you avoid putting any labels on yourself and committing to eating plans that are challenging for you to maintain. That's why we feel it's healthy to enjoy plenty of high-energy, fresh fruits; vegetables, including greens; and natural protein sources that come from plants. Organic tofu is a great source of protein, as long as it's certified non–genetically modified and you have no family or personal history of breast-health issues or medical issues that require you to avoid estrogen products. You can also get powders made from rice or pea protein. They are perfectly absorbable and rarely cause stomach upsets like dairy-based proteins. Your protein requirements are individual to you, so trust your body to guide you to how much is right for it.

Track Your Nutrition

You may have heard of *anaphylaxis,* which is a rapid, life-threatening allergic reaction to particular foods. Peanuts are a common cause, but any food could potentially be an allergen.

Our bodies also have a much subtler allergic system. These reactions take longer to occur, and the offending food is often overlooked as the trigger. For example, the glass of milk you had yesterday may not give you immediate inflammation. Instead, your body absorbs it and tries to break it down; however, it doesn't recognize it as food. Your body sees it as the enemy and, in the same way it responds to infections, creates a low level of inflammation in your digestive system. This sends out signals of distress more slowly than anaphylaxis, and it may take 24 to 48 to get symptoms, such as skin irritation, stuffy sinuses, headaches, or other signs of congestion. These are all due to that one glass of milk you had yesterday morning, but because it was more than 24 hours ago you don't make the connection.

This is why we feel so strongly about keeping a diet diary. It's more than just writing down *what* you ate for breakfast, lunch, and dinner; also record the *times* at which you ate them, how much water or other fluids you drank, what you were simultaneously doing, how you felt shortly afterward, and your energy levels. These things are very important to pay attention to.

DIET DIARY

	Time	What you ate or drank	How you felt	What you were doing while eating
Breakfast	7 A.M.	2 pieces of white toast with peanut butter	Bloated	Rushing to get ready for work
Morning snack				
Lunch				
Afternoon snack				
Dinner				
Evening snack				

The purpose of completing a diet diary, like the example given, is to clue you in to your own habits. For instance, it may show you that you aren't drinking as much water as you thought you were.

We've also spoken to many people who are convinced they eat a lot of fresh vegetables. Yet when they complete the diet diary, they discover that they're only eating them once or twice a week! Time moves quickly, and we can get busy with life. So it's understandable that your brain doesn't hold on to the memory of every meal you enjoy. That's why writing it down can really help. Many people have found that doing so actually helps them *change* their dietary habits. It leads them to make better choices—and results in the loss of a few unnecessary pounds.

Sometimes the changes that occur as you alter your diet may appear more subtly, rather than be immediately apparent. You might not notice them if you aren't particularly focused on detecting them. For example, you may find that when you don't have a good night's rest, you crave more carbohydrates the next day. It can be wonderfully useful to journal every day as you make these changes so you can see for yourself experientially when something works for you or doesn't.

Ask yourself:

- *Was today a normal day for me?*
- *Did I experience anything stressful?*
- *What were my relationship experiences like?*
- *Did I get a good night's sleep?*
- *Do I remember any dreams?*
- *Did I do meaningful work today?*
- *Did I take any supplements or herbs?*
- *Did I take any pharmaceutical medications?*
- *How much water did I drink?*
- *Did I have any cravings today?*

We encourage you to seize on those little things that show you that you're moving in the right direction. Look for changes in your energy levels, your mood, and how much work you complete over the course of the day. Notice how you handle challenging situations at home or with friends. All of these things are signs of how you're doing on a deeper level.

When you write down the foods and drinks you've consumed, reflect on how you feel about these dietary changes and how your outlook on life and intuitive abilities have been affected. Noting the levels of energy, motivation, and creativity you've experienced will show you very clearly that processed, artificial foods were starving you on an energetic level. You may have felt physically full, but emotionally, they were blocking you from the pace and the love you were craving.

Organics for Intuition

Sadly, through mass production, foods are developed and grown much faster than is natural. Many—including papayas and even pine-apples—are becoming genetically modified. What this means is that companies are altering the genetic makeup of these foods so that they can grow faster, be resistant to pests or various diseases, and even have a longer shelf life.

It sounds like a wonderful idea in the beginning, but then you realize that these fruits and vegetables are no longer what God created. Instead, they're a kind of human-made, Frankenstein-like creation. We think we're just eating a papaya, when we're eating something that is nothing like a papaya at all. With genetic modification, unhealthful pesticides are built right into the food. You can't wash them off or peel them away. What's even more frightening is that there has been so little research on genetically modified foods that we don't really know *what* happens when we eat them.

The angels have guided us to stay as far away from genetically engineered and genetically modified foods as possible. You can follow this guidance by always choosing organic options. The labeling of genetically modified food is different around the world. In some countries, the law says that companies must inform you. Yet, in others, there are no labeling requirements at all, making it much more difficult to know if your food is genetically modified or not. If you choose organic, then you can be assured that there's been no tampering with what you're eating. It's a real creation from Mother Nature and from God that your body will love.

We hear many people complain about the high cost of organic and nutritious food. Some say that they can't *afford* to eat healthfully. Our answer to this is that nutrition is an investment in health, which will save you money in the long run. In addition, because high-quality meals heighten your intuition and claircognizance, you will receive inspired ideas that will probably increase your income!

Besides, there are ways to eat healthfully on a budget, including:

- Growing your own organic produce. Even apartment dwellers can grow organic tomatoes, kale, and other food thanks to inexpensive hydroponic systems available online.

- Shopping at organic co-ops or farmers' markets.

- Creating a community organic garden.

- Learning to make your own meals from scratch, using organic ingredients.

- Subscribing to organic delivery services such as CSA (community-supported agriculture) boxes, which are cost saving compared to most grocery stores.

Fresh and Local

Many fruits are high in nutrients, but the important thing to keep in mind is that fresh is always best. The angels have taught us that we can no longer just look at a food and decide that it's going to give us an adequate amount of nutrition. What we mean by that is that it's difficult to, say, have an orange and be confident of its vitamin C content. That may have worked in the past, but due to today's production and storing techniques, we have no concept of how long ago that orange was plucked from the tree. Every second it's away from it ssource, it's losing nutritional value.

For many grocery stores and big chain supermarkets, those fruits and vegetables may have been picked from the tree or pulled from the ground months and months ago. That orange, which looks fresh and tasty sitting there on your plate, may actually have been stored for the last three or four months, locked in a freezer somewhere, and shipped from a different country. The vitamin C within that fruit may no longer be sufficient to sustain your body.

Of course, eating *any* fruit is far better than a candy bar, but the optimal choice is freshly picked, locally grown and produced foods. Find farmers' markets in your area—do a simple Internet search for the closest one to you. This is where farmers who are in your community sell their fresh produce—the fruits and vegetables they grow with care. Quite often these foods have been picked from the farm just a few days earlier! Their prices are frequently cheaper than the supermarket's, too.

In my naturopath practice, I (Robert) have treated several commercial farmers over the years. They tell me that they get very little money per item from supermarkets. So when you purchase your fruits and vegetables from the local farmers' market, you are also supporting these people. You'll often find organic produce at these locations, too. It's very, very fresh food and has a wonderful energy.

A benefit of choosing organic food is that it doesn't have a long shelf life. Why is that a good thing? Well, when you're buying organic and the produce *looks* nice, fresh, and tasty, then generally that means it *is*. There is always the chance that it could have been frozen and brought out later in the season, but this is less common. Please trust your intuition. Your own gut feelings will let you know which foods are going to be best for you.

The Way We Eat

When you eat something, you should do so for a reason. What many of us have been trained to do is look at the clock and decide that since it's 12 or 1 P.M., suddenly it's lunchtime, and that must mean that we're hungry. Now, having no food in your system over extended periods of time can slow down your metabolism. While this is okay during a detox process, it's not as effective for everyday maintenance. What we recommend you do is enjoy eating meals throughout the day.

Enjoy having breakfast, lunch, and dinner and a couple of healthy snacks to bridge those meals. We find that most people do really well if they have something small to eat every three to four hours instead of huge, further-apart meals that can take a long time to digest.

We like the idea of grazing throughout the day. That makes us feel lighter, too . . . and more intuitive, open, and uplifted, because our bodies are able to break down those foods much more easily. We have a stronger connection to our angels and to God, because we aren't feeling heavy, sluggish, or bloated. Eating high-vibration foods can enhance this connection even more.

The way in which you eat makes a significant difference when it comes to your intuition, as your eating style can also change how your body digests its food.

If you are calm and relaxed, meditating on the concept of peace, anything and everything you consume is going to be digested slowly. Your body will take its time, and each little molecule of nutrition is going to be absorbed. You'll look outside and you'll see beautiful butterflies and spontaneous rainbows, because everything in your world at that moment is going according to plan. Everything is happy . . . everything is love . . . because that's all that truly matters.

On the other hand, eating in a hurried manner creates a ripple effect of that energy and vibration. Your body feels like it has to rush to digest whatever it was you ate. It feels like there's this time crunch to get everything done. This will often make you feel nauseated and bloated.

Stressing and rushing never help us one little bit. In this frame of mind, we look to the outside world and only see more jobs for us to complete. We get in that mind-set that says, *Everything I'm experiencing now is going to continue indefinitely.*

When you eat in a harried, frantic manner, then everything you see outside has that matching energy and vibration. For example, you go out to the mailbox and collect the mail. There's nothing good in there, only bills. You meet some friends, who remind you of their invitations to events you forgot about, and you've got to squeeze these into your schedule. Your friend's birthday is among them, and now you've got the extra expense of buying a gift. All these things unfold this way just because of how you ate your meal. It really *is* affecting your perception of the world.

If you are rushing around, trying to get the children ready for school while also taking bites of a piece of toast, your body is going to react very differently compared with sitting down at the table, relaxed, feeling the warm sunshine coming through the window and settling in with a good book and your bowl of organic oatmeal.

When your body feels like it has to rush, it starts cutting corners, only doing the bare essentials in terms of its physical functions rather than the very best job it can do. It will feel a sense of urgency to digest and break down that meal. Due to the speed of the processing, you won't receive everything nutritionally that you could have. Not only that, but your intuition is going to switch off, because your endocrine system's priority has become digestion, which then takes precedence over everything else.

Thus the energy in which we consume food will also impact our intuition. When we choose to eat in a slow, relaxed, comfortable way, the world is a much brighter place.

Go Gradually

When I (Robert) first started taking the green dietary supplement spirulina, I did not like the taste at all. I was so inspired and motivated to try it because of the high nutritional value of this sea algae. I loved its healing properties, which I'd read about, but the flavor was unlike anything I'd encountered before. When I mixed the green powder with a little juice and took a sip, I instantly screwed my face up and thought, *Oh my goodness, there's no way I could ever drink this on a regular basis!*

But, rather than giving up immediately, I meditated on the spirulina. I asked God and my angels if this food was really going to serve a higher purpose for me. They assured me that it definitely would and explained that its emerald-green color resonates strongly with Archangel Raphael.

So I knew that I had to take spirulina. I asked the angels, "How am I going to make it more palatable?" What they taught me was that I should begin with a much lower dosage than what is recommended.

The suggested daily amount was around three grams—roughly equivalent to a teaspoon. The taste of that one heaped teaspoon of powder mixed with my small glass of juice was very strong and pungent, and I was never going to finish it. However, when I added just a quarter teaspoon to my juice, I found that I could barely even taste the spirulina! I did this for about a week; then afterward I upped the amount to half a teaspoon. Again, I did this for four or five days, until once more I increased the serving size.

Today, I can comfortably tolerate higher amounts of spirulina as a daily maintenance dose. It took a little time, but I'm so glad I started slowly and persisted with it. So if you try the different herbs, smoothies, and supplements discussed in the upcoming chapters and don't instantly enjoy the taste, consider a smaller amount and gradually work your way up.

If you make healthy choices today, your body will respond with a better tomorrow. Please don't become disheartened, thinking you can never make big changes. It simply happens one step at a time. You may begin by identifying healthy snacks that you enjoy (you'll find a few recipes in the next two chapters). Then you might decide to focus on breakfast, making a few small adjustments to that first meal of the day to increase the nutritional value. As your body begins to reward you for the high-energy foods you consume, you can embark on bigger changes, incorporating more of those high-vibrational foods at every single meal.

It's a gradual, step-by-step process. (In Part III we'll teach you how to overcome any obstacles to being the healthiest version of yourself.) Remember, though, that you're not going down this path alone. You have the loving support of God and your angels—and you have us here to help guide you through.

CHAPTER FIVE

Energizing Superfood Snacks and Soups to Jump-start Your Intuition

There are trillions of cells within your precious body, and each one of them needs proper nourishment to maintain a high level of energy and vitality. That's why you should consume only foods and beverages that match up and align with your true intentions. If you eat high-energy, high-vibrational foods, then cells will mimic that energy and vibration. As you eat and drink different things, your body is absorbing the life force, the true essence and energy, of those substances. This is circulated to your cells, and that is what influences your mood, your motivation, and your creativity . . . and, of course, it has a very real impact on your intuition.

This is why when we eat high-energy foods, we feel alive—we feel awakened! Conversely, if we eat artificial substances, or human-made foods, we can feel sluggish, tired, and maybe even depressed.

Every 90 days your body has a complete new supply of red blood cells. So, 90 days from right now, every single red blood cell within your circulatory system is going to be different. Your body is constantly re-creating itself in response to the direction your life is currently headed. This is a true blessing. It means that today you can make healthier choices than you did yesterday, and by tomorrow your body will already have begun to respond.

So, instead of consuming fast food, try the superfoods in this chapter. You'll be amazed by how much clearer your intuition becomes in just a short time.

Kale

Topping the list of superfoods we love is kale. This fantastic green leafy vegetable is jam-packed with nutrients.

Kale is quite low in calories (approximately 36 per cup) and high in fiber. The cleansing properties of the fiber help to . . .

- . . . remove toxins from your digestive tract.

- . . . capture unhealthy fats and pull them out of your system.

- . . . regulate blood-sugar levels.

- . . . reduce cholesterol levels, thereby relieving pressure on the heart.

The emerald-green color eases the area around the heart on a physical level and resonates with the heart chakra, healing us emotionally, too.

The kale itself doesn't have any fat, which helps account for its low calorie count. But don't be fooled. Just because it isn't high in calories doesn't mean it's not nutrient dense. There are around *80 different nutrients* found in kale.

There are so many benefits from just one simple food:

- Per calorie, kale contains more **iron** than beef. The iron in kale is highly absorbable by the body. (Another leafy green, spinach, contains iron, too, but it has high levels of oxalates. These bind to the iron—and also calcium— and make it challenging for the body to break it down.)

- Kale is very high in **vitamin K,** which works to maintain your blood consistency so it's not too thick and not too thin, and which may help combat various cancers. Vitamin K is also important for bone health and can boost calcium absorption.

- Kale is rich in **vitamin A,** which helps balance your immune system and is healing to the skin. It can break down mucus congestion and clear sinus issues.

- Kale also provides a great deal of **vitamin C** to boost your immune system. Vitamin C helps rebuild your body's energy stores as well.

- Kale can help reduce inflammation, as it contains soothing **omega-3 fatty acids.**

- Kale is a great source of **calcium** and has more available calcium per calorie than milk.

- Kale even contains **protein** to provide you with energy and help your body build and repair all its tissues.

This powerful green vegetable is so versatile. You can serve it in salads. You can stir-fry it. You can steam it. You can add it to soups. You can even mix it into smoothies, which is one of our favorite ways to enjoy it.

Substituting kale for lettuce in a salad works beautifully. You pull the soft leaves from the hard, tough stem of the plant and then gently massage the kale. When I (Robert) first saw "massaged kale" listed on a restaurant menu, I thought it was the most hilarious thing I'd ever heard of! I wondered, *What on earth does that mean?*

Well, it means exactly what it implies. I tried it on my own. To my surprise, massaging the kale made it much easier to eat. You just lightly squash the cabbage-like leaves between your hands, and it will break down some of the toughness. It gives the kale more of a lettuce/spinach kind of texture. You can massage the leaves with a fat such as fresh avocado or with oils, for wonderful tenderness and flavor. In my research, I found that this technique helps release any bitterness that the kale leaf may contain, so it makes it a little sweeter and tastier.

We also love to add the tiny, sweet seeds from inside pomegranates to our kale salads, because they are rich in vitamins. This high-vibrational fruit just beams with joy. You can also pop the seeds into your smoothies or juices for a dose of "happiness." We will be talking about how to make green smoothies a little later on, but you can start enjoying kale right away with the following two recipes.

KALE SALAD

This lovely salad features massaged kale paired with the interesting flavor and texture of pomegranate seeds. Using the fruit's juice as a dressing tops off an uplifting and refreshing meal.

Ingredients:
2 cups kale with stems removed
½ avocado
Seeds from ½ pomegranate
1 tbsp. sunflower seeds
Juice from remaining ½ pomegranate

In a salad bowl, massage the avocado into the kale leaves to soften. Sprinkle the pomegranate seeds and sunflower seeds throughout. Dress with the juice from the remaining half of the pomegranate

KALE CHIPS

This healthy snack has a bit of crunch—just another fun way to include nutrition-loaded kale in your diet.

Ingredients:
1 bunch kale
1 tsp. Celtic or Himalayan sea salt
2 tbsp. olive oil
Herbs and spices of choice for seasoning

Carefully tear the kale leaves from the stalk, leaving them in big pieces. Add the leaves and other ingredients to a large bowl. Gently massage the kale and make sure every leaf is coated.

Place on a baking tray lined with parchment paper, and set in an oven at 250°F/120°C. You may wish to leave the door open to prevent the oven from getting too hot—the aim here is to dry the kale, not burn it. Turn the leaves over after 15 minutes, and cook for an additional 15 minutes.

Remove the tray from the oven and allow to cool. You can season the leaves with a variety of herbs and spices, including paprika or chili powder. You might even try dipping them in some homemade salsa!

Sprouts

When you think of a plant's life cycle and how it begins to grow, the sprout stage is one of the most energy-intense intervals. Courageously breaking through that seedpod and making its way into the world takes so much determination and fortitude.

Sprouts are, quite literally, seeds that have just begun to grow. Alfalfa sprouts are the most widely known, but there are also many other kinds—mung bean, chickpea, and broccoli, just to name a few. The nutrient density, energy, and vibration of sprouts are all very high. We enjoy them in our salads and smoothies.

Sprouts give us brand-new life force from the plant. We wondered if it was okay to eat them, given that this *is* newly created life. When we asked the angels, they said that we must consume sprouts because they are so powerfully nutritious and also wonderfully uplifting to our energy. Mother Nature and God aren't upset about our harvesting their creation for food. Instead, they endorse incorporating sprouts into our diets to give us the energy to go the distance. If we can move forward feeling uplifted, positive, and safe, we've achieved the true goal that all life in the natural world is here for.

You can enjoy sprouts in many different ways, even as snacks during the day. For example, mix them in with a little hummus to create a wonderfully delicious spread on crackers. Some varieties are more flavorful than others, but the taste doesn't matter as much as the freshness and vitality of the plant.

How to Grow Your Own Sprouts

Growing your own sprouts is easy and fun to do. You have a couple of options: purchase a sprouting kit from your local health-food store (or online) or create your own with a glass jar and a piece of muslin cloth or cheesecloth.

You can purchase regular organic sunflower seeds, pepitas, mung beans, chickpeas, lentils, quinoa, and several others from your health-food store; or, alternatively, you can buy seeds, grains, or legumes that have been packaged specifically for the purpose of sprouting. They amount to the same thing, and you'll have to trust your intuition as to which type is the freshest. That being said, the sprouting section of the store will often have varieties that aren't available elsewhere, so be sure to check it out.

Begin by adding some of the seeds, grains, or legumes to your glass jar. Fill with water, cover with the kit's lid or your piece of cloth (a rubber band is useful to hold it in place), and let sit for 8 to 12 hours. Now, drain the water by simply inverting the jar (the cloth or sprouting lid will hold in your sprouts). Rinse well by filling with fresh water, shaking, and emptying. Repeat this a few times before setting the jar upside down on a sunny windowsill so that any excess water can drain out.

Every 8 to 12 hours, again rinse the sprouts by filling the jar with fresh water, shaking, and draining, each time getting as much excess water out as possible. After three to four days of absorbing the energy from the sun, your sprouts will begin to appear! Give them another really good rinsing before enjoying them. You can store them in the fridge for a few more days.

When you get inspired about sprouting, you may choose to have several sprout jars growing at once. This way you can alternate which sprouts you enjoy, as well as have a constant supply!

Satisfying Soup

In order for your intuition to be fully activated and awakened, your body needs to be filled with nourishing, high-vibrational foods. At times, this might seem like a struggle. You may feel that you're constantly sitting down to eat the same meal again and again. Doing the same thing repeatedly is not only boring; it's bad for your body.

We encourage you to rotate your foods, including leafy green vegetables, because your body craves an assortment. When you focus on one or two foods to the exclusion of other options and have them every day, you miss out on important nutrients and your body can become upset.

That's where soups come in.

Let's be honest. You probably don't *love* every single vegetable, and that's okay! Pretend for a moment that you've sat down to some steamed zucchini—not your favorite. You look at it and push it around the plate, trying your best to work up the willpower to take a bite. Unfortunately, this rarely happens.

With a soup, you can add loads of nutritious vegetables, some of which you may not even care for. Blend the soup up and enjoy all sorts of wonderful goodness—without any disagreeable flavors.

Soup Simplicity

Soups are so simple to make. You quite literally just throw a whole heap of different veggies and herbs into a pot. Cover with some water, and allow to boil for an hour or two. When the vegetables become tender, the soup is ready.

We like to add in the extra step of blending our soups. A puree is much easier for your body to absorb. Think of how many times you chew your food before you swallow it. Maybe even go grab a bite to eat right now, and test yourself.

On average, most of us will chew each mouthful of food fewer than ten times. Naturopathic guidelines suggest that we should chew at least *30 times* before we swallow. Chewing your food well is going to break it down to the smallest size possible. When you swallow, your body can easily digest all the nutrients the meal contains. Try chewing each mouthful of food 30 times and notice just how long it takes you to eat something. Your jaw will probably become sore because it's unused to utilizing those muscles for such an extended period.

Think of raw carrot sticks. Carrot is quite a hard vegetable, isn't it? You generally chew it a couple of times and swallow. Now your digestive system has to process big chunks that it can't possibly break down. The body will do its best, but it's not going to absorb all the goodness of the carrot.

Now think of this scenario: That carrot has been blended and pureed so that the whole vegetable has turned to mush. It has been stewing for an hour or longer. You can now easily absorb everything the carrot has to give you. The small particle size means your body can extract more nutrition.

You might be thinking, *How can a food that's been cooked for so long be so high-energy and high-vibrational?*

Well, when your vegetables are organic, the energy from the time and care it's taken to grow them comes through in the meal.

What we'll often do is create big pots with loads and loads of vegetables fresh from our local farmers' markets. Or we'll put cut vegetables in a high-speed blender to make a naturally creamy soup. We then allow it to cook for however long it needs.

We keep some of the soup in the refrigerator to feed our families for the next couple of days. We put the remainder into BPA-free containers and store them in the freezer. Even after being frozen for a month or two, the soup is still high-energy and so wonderfully nourishing.

The fiber derived from the soup, from all those beautiful vegetables, acts like a pipe cleaner that clears out your digestive system. It pulls away toxic compounds and any poorly digested substances and flushes them out of your body. Research has also shown that high-fiber diets can help reduce cholesterol. By releasing these toxins, you'll experience an increased sense of clarity.

When you feel sluggish, tired, or bloated after eating, it's because the meal was dense and heavy. It may take your body an extra hour or two to break it down. When that happens, messages from your own Divine guidance become fuzzy. It's like you've got cotton balls in your ears. Of course, your angels don't go away. In truth they *never* leave your side. It's just that your ability to hear them is no longer as acute.

When you eat soup, you feel light, energized, and refreshed. You don't feel bloated and uncomfortable, because your body instantly goes to work digesting, as soon as you start the meal.

In fact, in an experiment, a group of people were given a plate full of vegetables and a glass of water, while a second group received the same amount of food blended all together in a soup. Interestingly, the group who had the soup felt fuller, reporting that they remained satisfied for longer.

The researchers drew the conclusion that when we don't chew our food very well, it sinks to the bottom of the stomach and the water floats on top. Those food particles go through first, and the water quickly follows. Then we feel hungry again. In the case of a soup, it's filling up the stomach with diffuse particles suspended in liquid.

Your stomach recognizes that every part of that meal is food. It's vegetables. It's fiber. It's herbs and it's water. The entire digestive system is working to absorb the nutrients, the vibration, and the energy from what you've just eaten. At the same time, you're unlocking all of the potential nourishment from those organic vegetables. That's why soup makes you feel fuller and more satisfied.

Raw Soups

We also like to make what are called *raw soups.* Now, for these, we actually use friction from the spinning blades of a high-powered blender, such as the Vitamix, to heat the food. With this technique, you can throw a couple of whole vegetables, a tomato or two, and a little bit of water into the blender and leave it on for eight to ten minutes. That's enough to heat up the food and make it into a steaming soup.

In truth, the food is still raw. It's not "cooked" like a traditional soup, where it has been brought to a high heat and simmered for hours. This raw soup has a different energy altogether, as you're also bringing in some of the freshness of the high-vibrational ingredients.

We like to rotate the different ways in which we enjoy soup. We have some raw soups and some cooked. Then, when we're short on time to prepare a meal, we'll pull one of our storage containers out of the freezer and heat the contents up on the stove, and in 15 to 20 minutes, we've got a delicious, healthy soup to enjoy.

Water

Making soup is like creating a magical mixture of energy and nutrition. The flavors from the different vegetables and herbs are infused into the water, lending their healing vibrations to the broth. That's why we really don't like boiling vegetables. By straining the water, you're sending the best part of the meal down the drain. You might as well throw those vegetables in the garbage and drink the broth, because it's probably got more nutrition in it.

Choose the best-quality water you can to make your soup. Depending on where you are in the world, the tap water may very well contain fluoride. Many different studies have shown the negative side effects of fluoride. We're told that the fluoride is helping strengthen our teeth, but what's shocking is that it makes absolutely no difference. Research comparing countries that have fluoride in their water with those that don't has demonstrated that they have the same prevalence of dental cavities. Fluoride is also a toxic chemical, linked to many diseases and health issues, including the growth of some tumors.

The best way to remove fluoride from your tap water is through reverse osmosis. This is a filtration system you can have installed in your home. You could also buy bottled water, ideally in glass bottles, without added fluoride.

If you're going to create a high-vibrational, intuition-boosting soup, then please use natural springwater or reverse-osmosis filtered water. By cooking your soup in a nourishing base, you enhance the quality. When you eat something that has a toxic compound in it, of course that's going to dampen your psychic abilities. So take fluoride out of the equation!

Before you throw in all the vegetables, take a moment to infuse that pot of water with positive energy. Hold your hands just above it and close your eyes for a moment. You might find it helpful to briskly rub your palms together for a few seconds first. This awakens the chakras in your hands, making them more sensitive. Next, visualize a purifying white light coming out through your palms and radiating into the water. See every molecule responding to that energy, raising its vibration. Then, as you consume the soup, the energy you absorb will be magnified.

You can also use this moment to infuse the soup with a specific prayer or intention. If you'd like to awaken your clairvoyance, see yourself receiving clear visions as you send that intention into the soup. If you'd like to have a stronger connection with God and your angels, imagine them standing right beside you and communicating with you in a meaningful way. If you'd like to attract more love or find a supportive spiritual group, envision yourself in a perfectly balanced soul-mate relationship or among like-minded friends.

Water is such a wonderful vessel for energy. It retains a magical "memory" of the vibration it was infused with. If you send love into your water, then the water will respond in kind. This is why it's so important to be peaceful and open as you prepare your food. If you create a soup (or any meal) in an agitated state, then you're going to introduce stress into that meal. Every time you take the soup out of the freezer, you'll pick up on the vibration of stress. Isn't it so much better to cook in a peaceful state, to feel connected and loved, so that every time you consume that soup, you feel those wonderful, positive things?

Legumes

You can add extra ingredients to your soup and make it your own. Allow your creativity to flow freely. We love to just throw in everything we have on hand that we feel guided to use and see what happens.

Sometimes we'll add legumes, like beans and lentils. There are two ways you can consider including these:

1. **Buy dried legumes.** Soak the beans in a big bowl of water for at least 24 hours, because they have to rehydrate themselves. Another important reason for this soaking period is that beans and legumes naturally contain traces of toxins, chemicals the plant produces to ward off pests and bugs. If you're eating large amounts of legumes, you don't want to take in any of those toxic elements. By soaking them in water for a day or more, you allow the toxicity to be drawn out.

Afterward, rinse well and add the beans and legumes to the soup. Gently simmer for an hour to an hour and a half, making sure that they're nice and tender.

2. What's often easier is to **use canned beans and lentils.** You can keep them in the cupboard, ready to go, without needing preparation a day ahead of time. You can just grab a few cans out of the cupboard and make your meal on the fly.

Many canned beans and lentils have added salt in the water. So be sure to rinse them really, really well. Don't drink the water, because it could contain some of those toxic compounds we just mentioned. After thoroughly rinsing, we feel guided to place those beans in a bowl of clean water, just like we would dried beans. Often, though, we feel half an hour to an hour is enough soak time—just long enough to help pull out that added salt or any toxins.

It's really important to choose canned products that have no BPA in the lining. (You'll notice there's a plastic film inside the can that protects the beans from coming into contact with the metal.) If the can contains BPA, this chemical can actually create hormone imbalances within your body. This is not exclusive to women, either, affecting men just as strongly.

The brand Amy's guarantees that none of their canned products contain BPA. It's something you'll want to be aware of. You're making the soup to raise your vibration and enhance your intuition. Therefore you'll want each meal to be as clean and chemical-free as possible.

Here are two soup recipes, perfect for a light meal or snack. You simply chop up the ingredients and pop them all into a large pot, and you will have a wonderful supply of delicious, nourishing soup!

VEGETABLE SOUP

Ingredients:
1 head green cabbage
3 parsnips
1 cup mushrooms
5 carrots
5 spring onions
5 celery sticks
2 zucchini
4 stalks kale
5 cups chopped tomatoes (good-quality organic canned tomatoes are fine)
3 tsp. chopped garlic
5 tsp. dried parsley
5 tsp. dried basil
1½ tsp. chili powder
4 vegetable-based, salt-reduced stock/bouillon cubes

Chop up all vegetables, then add ingredients to a pot with 12 cups of water and simmer for 1–2 hours.

SQUASH SOUP

Ingredients:
2 butternut squash, peeled and cubed
4 cups vegetable stock
½ tsp. minced fresh ginger
1 cup Cashew Sour Cream (recipe on page 83)

Roast squash in a 350°F/180°C oven for 45 minutes or until tender. Add squash and other ingredients to a pot with 2 cups of water, and simmer 1–2 hours.

High-vibration food allows your intuition to open. In contrast, artificial sweeteners, artificial colors, and just generally fake food clog up your energy centers, blocking the ability to receive messages from your angels. It makes it very hard to hear Divine guidance! By eating real food—especially nourishing superfoods and filling soups—you ensure that the channels to your intuition remain clear.

CHAPTER SIX

Nourishing Nuts, Seeds, and "Mylks"

Nuts and seeds are a healthy snack, as they contain protein, good fats, and fiber. However, many also contain enzyme inhibitors that may put extra strain on your body. These inhibitors bind to enzymes and block or slow down their actions. If you eat a large amount of raw nuts, you may feel heavy, as your digestive system struggles to break them down. They also contain small amount of phytic acid, which the body is unable to process.

Activated Nuts and Seeds

By "activating" nuts and seeds, you release enzyme inhibitors and make all the valuable nutrition easier for your body to absorb. You can activate a variety of nuts and seeds, and here are our guided recommendations as to which are best activated:

- Almonds
- Peanuts
- Hazelnuts
- Macadamias
- Walnuts

- Pumpkin seeds (pepitas)
- Sunflower seeds

The process is simple, and you can easily do it yourself at home. Many health-food stores sell activated nuts, but they are considerably more expensive.

Place the nuts (or seeds) into a large bowl. Cover with filtered water or fresh springwater. Next, add a teaspoon of Celtic or Himalayan sea salt. (The salt helps with the activation process to release the enzyme inhibitors.) Stir well to ensure the salt is dissolved and all of the nuts are covered with water. Leave to soak for 12 hours, then drain the nuts and rinse them really well. Now, dry them in the oven at the lowest setting possible, for as long as it takes for them to become crisp again.

You can now enjoy these healthy treats as snacks, in your smoothies, and in salads.

Note: Be mindful of the higher oil content of some nuts, such as macadamias and walnuts; they don't require soaking for as long.

Cashews

You may have noticed that cashews are not on the "activated" list. It might come as a surprise to you to learn that they are not a nut at all. Cashews are actually the seed of a fruit! They don't require activation, as they don't contain the enzyme inhibitors. So you can whip up the following recipe with comparatively minimal prep time!

CASHEW SOUR CREAM

This is a great sauce for almost any dish. It works well with most flavors and can even be used as a creamy salad dressing.

Ingredients:
2 cups soaked cashews (soaking for 5 hours creates a beautiful, smooth "cream")
2 tbsp. coconut oil
2 tbsp. lemon juice
2 tsp. salt
½ cup water

Place all the ingredients into your blender and start on a low speed. Depending on the type of machine you have, you may need to stop and stir the mixture every now and then. Increase the speed to medium and continue to blend until you have a creamy, smooth sauce. You can store this in the fridge for a couple of days in a glass container. This recipe will yield approximately 1½ cups.

Chia Seeds

Chia seeds, with among the highest omega-3 content of all plant foods, are wonderful sources of energy—giving you a far greater pick-me-up than any carbohydrates, sugar, or caffeine ever will. Traditionally they were used by the Aztecs to provide endurance over long periods of time.

We suggest briefly soaking chia seeds. Add a tablespoon of chia seeds to a cup of water. Allow the seeds to soak for 10 to 15 minutes and you'll see them expand and take on a gel consistency, evidence of the wonderful essential fatty acids that your body wants. By soaking those chia seeds, you allow them to be easily digested and absorbed.

Now you can add them to a smoothie! Blend them up—you won't even notice that they're in there. The smoothie will be filling and highly nutritious. Or try the following recipe for a mouthwatering treat.

TASTY CHIA PUDDING

This is a simple and delicious way to include more chia in your diet. It brings some wonderful sweetness, so it's perfect for dessert!

Ingredients:

1 cup coconut "mylk" or any of our other nut or seed mylks (see next section)

2 tbsp. maple syrup

1 tsp. alcohol-free, organic vanilla extract

½ tsp. cinnamon

½ tsp. nutmeg

2 tbsp. chia seeds

1 ripe banana

This recipe looks great when served in a glass. Add the mylk, maple syrup, vanilla, cinnamon, nutmeg, and chia to the glass. Stir until well blended. Place the glass in the fridge to chill. After 30 minutes, stir the mixture again to evenly distribute the chia seeds. Now, allow it to set for a further 4 hours in the fridge. Mash the banana and gently stir into the chia pudding.

You can transform the flavor of this simple chia pudding by changing the type of mylk or fruit. Mango, strawberries, blueberries, and peach are some of our favorites.

Nut and Seed "Mylks"

As we've discussed, your body was never designed to digest dairy products, which create inflammation and irritation in your digestive tract. Often the reactions to dairy are slow and subtle. It may take 24 to 48 hours for ingestion of dairy to negatively impact you, which makes it challenging to identify the cause of the aggravation.

Plant-based "mylks" are much more nourishing to your body. (We use the word *mylk* to differentiate from dairy, and because it's common in natural health circles.) They provide abundant vitamins, minerals, and healthy oils, as well as protein and fiber. Sometimes it can be too much effort to eat nuts and seeds by the handful, so that's why we love getting their wonderful nutrition through mylk. Nut and seed mylks are quite simple to make. With just a little advance planning, you can have fresh mylk to use in your smoothies, cereals, or desserts.

It may be tempting to pick up premade mylk from the store, as many markets now carry a variety. However, like all prepackaged foods, it may contain preservatives, emulsifiers, and sweeteners. We've seen some popular brands that include the harmful additive carrageenan in their products. Carrageenan is a natural compound, but it has been found to cause irritation and inflammation in the stomach. It triggers a response from the immune system and has been linked to gastric ulceration and even cancer. Since it's a natural extract, it may be present even in organic brands. The purpose of the additive is to ensure the mylk doesn't separate. So, if you can bear the burden of having to shake your mylk, you can avoid it altogether.

Variety really is the secret to a happy and healthy life, and plant-based mylks are no exception. We encourage you to alternate which mylks you make and avoid relying on just one. Each has unique nutrition and helps you differently on an energetic level. By rotating the types of mylk you make, you'll receive a well-balanced assortment of healing nourishment.

You'll see that we choose to sweeten most of our mylks with natural additions. This is personal preference and not necessary. We find the added sweetness gives the mylk a creamier taste and makes for delicious smoothies! Medjool dates are a fabulous, healthy source of sweetness, as is maple syrup. Please buy real, organic, sustainably harvested maple syrup (maple-flavor syrup simply won't do). There are many other syrups available such as agave, yacón, and coconut. However, maple syrup has one of the lowest levels of fructose compared with the others. This means the sugars are used by your body more slowly, preventing blood-sugar spikes. Maple syrup also has some nutrients in it, as well as antioxidants.

The following recipes each yield approximately four 1-cup servings.

SUNFLOWER MYLK

We love the uplifting energy of sunflowers. It's so hard to resist smiling when you look at their big, happy faces. The sunflower reminds you to shine your light. It comforts you with the reassurance that the worst is behind you, and now you only have positive things ahead. It empowers you, boosts your confidence, and illuminates the joy within your soul. When you make Sunflower Mylk, it's like drinking in golden sunshine!

This beautiful mylk is rich in zinc for healthy hair, skin, and nails. This mineral also balances your immune system, heals your nervous system, and can promote relaxation.

Ingredients:
1 cup raw sunflower seeds (hulled)
1¼ tsp. Celtic or Himalayan sea salt (divided)
3 cups filtered water or natural springwater, plus a bowlful for soaking
1 tsp. alcohol-free, organic vanilla extract (optional)
2 tbsp. maple syrup (optional)

Soak the sunflower seeds in a large bowl of fresh water, with 1 tsp. salt, for at least 12 hours. Drain the seeds and rinse really well. Add the soaked sunflower seeds, 3 cups water, and ¼ tsp. salt to your blender. If your blender has variable speeds, start off slow for 10 seconds before increasing to high. Blend for about a minute until all the seeds are broken down and you're left with a mylk. Taste now, and if you like, add the vanilla extract and maple syrup for sweetness and to balance out the sunflower-seed flavor.

Pour your Sunflower Mylk into a glass bottle or jar with a lid, and store in the fridge. It will keep for two days refrigerated.

PEPITA (PUMPKIN SEED) MYLK

Pepitas are filled with healthy protein. This mylk gives you strength and courage. It supports you when faced with challenging circumstances. Keep your faith and know that you will be okay. By retaining the pulp in the mylk, you are getting all the goodness from the pepitas, including iron, zinc, and amino acids.

Ingredients:

1 cup raw pepitas (hulled)

1¼ tsp. Celtic or Himalayan sea salt (divided)

3 cups filtered water or natural springwater, plus a bowlful for soaking

1 tsp. alcohol-free, organic vanilla extract (optional)

2 medjool dates (pitted) (optional)

Soak the pepitas in a large bowl of fresh water, with 1 tsp. salt, for at least 6 hours. Drain the seeds and rinse really well. Place the soaked pepitas, 3 cups water, and ¼ tsp. salt in your blender. If your blender has variable speeds, start off slow for 10 seconds before increasing to high. Blend for about a minute until all the seeds are broken down and you're left with a mylk. Due to the pigmentation of the pumpkin seeds, you'll end up with a slightly green mixture. Taste it now, and if you like, add the vanilla extract and dates for sweetness, before blending some more. This helps make the mylk a little more palatable but is optional.

Pour your Pepita Mylk into a glass bottle or jar with a lid, and store in the fridge. It will keep for two days refrigerated.

HAZELNUT MYLK

Hazelnut Mylk has a buttery, almost dessert-like feel to it. The flavor is reminiscent of chocolate (and pairs beautifully with cacao). Hazelnuts do have a higher fat content than other nuts, but provided that you aren't exclusively having this type of mylk, your intake should be fine. It's rich in vitamin E; is a strong antioxidant; and contains B vitamins, as well as calcium, zinc, and iron.

Drinking this mylk is like giving yourself a comforting, warm hug. It assures you that all is well, and even though you may not understand why things are currently happening the way they are, all is in perfect, Divine order. Your prayers have been heard, and God and your angels are sending you their love.

Ingredients:
1 cup raw hazelnuts
1¼ tsp. Celtic or Himalayan sea salt (divided)
2 cups filtered water or natural springwater, plus a bowlful for soaking
1 tsp. alcohol-free, organic vanilla extract
3 tbsp. maple syrup,

Soak the hazelnuts in a large bowl of fresh water, with 1 tsp. salt, for 12 hours. Drain the nuts and rinse really well. Put the soaked hazelnuts, 2 cups water, and ¼ tsp. salt into your blender. This mylk tastes better with a hint of sweetness, so add the vanilla and maple syrup now, too. If your blender has variable speeds, start off slow for 10 seconds before increasing to high. Blend for about a minute until all the nuts are broken down and you're left with a mylk.

Pour your Hazelnut Mylk into a glass bottle or jar with a lid, and store in the fridge. It will keep for two days refrigerated.

BRAZIL-NUT MYLK

Brazil nuts are a great source of selenium, a strong antioxidant reputed to prevent many kinds of cancer. Certain areas of the world (Australia is one example) have poor levels of selenium in the soil. Your fruits and vegetables can only get their mineral content from the soil, so if there's very little present, the foods will be mineral deficient, too. You can "import" selenium into your diet with these South American nuts. Brazil nuts have a high concentration of oil, so they are prone to going rancid. Be sure to buy recently packaged Brazil nuts (you can tell they're fresher if there is a long time before their expiration date) and store them in your fridge.

When you feel like you need a break away from everything, reach for Brazil-Nut Mylk. It helps you forget your troubles and find a sense of peace.

Ingredients:
1 cup raw Brazil nuts
1¼ tsp. Celtic or Himalayan sea salt (divided)
4 cups filtered water or natural springwater, plus a bowlful for soaking
2 tsp. cinnamon powder
2 tbsp. maple syrup (optional)

Soak the Brazil nuts in a large bowl of fresh water, with 1 tsp. salt, for 5 hours. Due to their higher oil content, you don't want them to soak for too long. Drain the nuts and rinse really well. Put the soaked Brazil nuts, 4 cups water, ¼ tsp. salt, and cinnamon into your blender. (The cinnamon gives this mylk a great taste and also helps balance blood sugar.) If your blender has variable speeds, start off slow for 10 seconds before increasing to high. Blend for about a minute until all the nuts are broken down and you're left with a mylk. Now, you can add some maple syrup if you feel it needs a little additional sweetness.

Pour your Brazil-Nut Mylk into a glass bottle or jar with a lid, and store in the fridge. It will keep for two days refrigerated.

CASHEW MYLK

Cashews create a creamy, rich mylk that is delicious and decadent. As we mentioned, although they are often referred to as nuts, technically they are seeds. Cashews, while still being highly nutritious, aren't like other nuts and seeds. It's rare to find truly "raw" cashews because they need to be steamed to coax them out of their toxic shell. So most so-called raw cashews have been steamed, but not roasted. Because the cashews aren't in their natural state, we recommend Cashew Mylk as an occasional treat rather than as a staple mylk. It makes a delicious smoothie base and adds a great creamy flavor to muesli and cereal.

Cashew Mylk removes blocks to hearing your intuition. It opens all your channels of communication to allow for effortless insight. This is a great mylk to have before meditation, writing, or teaching.

Ingredients:
1 cup "raw" cashews
1¼ tsp. Celtic or Himalayan sea salt (divided)
3 cups filtered water or natural springwater, plus a bowlful for soaking

Soak the cashews in a large bowl of fresh water, with 1 tsp. salt, for 5 hours. Cashews are a softer seed, so they don't require as long to soak. Drain them and rinse really well. Put the soaked cashews, 3 cups water, and ¼ tsp. salt into your blender. Blend for about a minute until all the seeds are broken down and you're left with a mylk.

Pour your Cashew Mylk into a glass bottle or jar with a lid, and store in the fridge. It will keep for two days refrigerated.

BROWN-RICE MYLK

Rice milk can be an acquired taste. Most store-bought versions have an unusual aftertaste that can make them unpleasant. However, if you are sensitive to nuts, you may find this dairy alternative more appropriate. Rice—technically a seed—is also gluten-free. We add a little sweetness to this mylk to make it more enjoyable.

Brown-Rice Mylk helps you speak up and say what's on your mind. It gives you unwavering faith in your gut feelings, shields you from negative energies, and strengthens your auric field.

Ingredients:
½ cup cooked brown rice

2 cups filtered water or natural springwater

A pinch of Celtic or Himalayan sea salt

3 medjool dates (pitted)

1 tsp. cinnamon powder

1 tsp. maple syrup

To make this mylk, you need just a small amount of cooked brown rice.

(You may wish to cook a batch for dinner and save some of it to make the mylk. Using 1 cup dry rice will yield 3 to 4 cups cooked. Before cooking, soak rice in a bowl of water with a teaspoon of salt for a minimum of 12 hours; if you allow it to soak for 24 hours, it's much lighter and creamier. Once soaked, drain and rinse well. Place the rice and 2 cups water in a pot, bring to a boil, then reduce to a simmer and cover. Once the rice is tender, after approximately 20 minutes, it's ready. Set aside and allow to cool.)

Put the cooked rice, 2 cups water, pinch of salt, dates, cinnamon, and maple syrup into your blender. Blend for about a minute until all the rice is broken down and you're left with a mylk.

Pour your Brown-Rice Mylk into a glass bottle or jar with a lid, and store in the fridge. It will keep for two days refrigerated.

MACADAMIA MYLK

Macadamias are rich, creamy, and just downright delicious! They're a nice source of protein, B vitamins, and manganese. They also contain healthy oils that nourish the heart and cardiovascular system.

This mylk brings your focus back to love. It's a heart-centered energy, and everything that comes from love is healing in nature. It awakens your clairvoyance, helping you have psychic visions in your mind and in the physical world. It's wonderful for attracting romantic relationships, balanced business partnerships, compassionate therapists, and trustworthy clients.

Ingredients:
1 cup raw macadamia nuts
1¼ tsp. Celtic or Himalayan sea salt (divided)
3 cups filtered water or natural springwater, plus a bowlful for soaking
1 tsp. alcohol-free, organic vanilla extract (optional)
2 tbsp. maple syrup (optional)

Soak the macadamias in a large bowl of fresh water, with 1 tsp. salt, for 5 hours. Macadamias don't require a long soaking time. Drain the nuts and rinse really well. Put the soaked macadamias, 3 cups water, and ¼ tsp. salt into your blender. Blend for about a minute until all the nuts are broken down and you're left with a mylk. Taste now and, if desired, you can mix in the vanilla extract and maple syrup.

Pour your Macadamia Mylk into a glass bottle or jar with a lid, and store in the fridge. It will keep for two days refrigerated.

ALMOND MYLK

Of all the plant-based mylks, almond is the most commonly known. While it can be found at almost any supermarket without too much trouble, we recommend making your own to ensure the highest quality, best nutritional value, and appropriate sweetness. It's simple, and so versatile that you can use it in smoothies, with cereal, or as a treat on its own!

Almond Mylk clears and balances your hundreds of chakras, with special attention to the seven major chakras running up the midline of your body. Thus, it balances multiple issues associated with these energy centers, including safety, security, money, creativity, your wants and desires, self-esteem and confidence, love, communication, intuition, and your connection to God. When you drink this mylk, you help restore harmony in all areas of your life.

Ingredients:
1 cup raw almonds
1¼ tsp. Celtic or Himalayan sea salt (divided)
3 cups filtered water or natural springwater, plus a bowlful for soaking
1 tsp. alcohol-free, organic vanilla extract (optional)
2 medjool dates (pitted) (optional)

Soak the almonds in a large bowl of fresh water, with 1 tsp. salt, for at least 12 hours. Drain the nuts and rinse really well. Put the soaked almonds, 3 cups water, and ¼ tsp. salt into your blender. Blend for about a minute until all the nuts are broken down and you're left with a mylk. Taste, and if you'd like a little more sweetness and flavor, add the vanilla and dates before blending again, until a smooth consistency is achieved.

Pour your Almond Mylk into a glass bottle or jar with a lid, and store in the fridge. It will keep for two days refrigerated.

The next chapter focuses on more blended creations to nourish you physically and spiritually.

CHAPTER SEVEN

Spiritual-Psychic Smoothies and Juices

Fresh organic fruits and vegetables, of course, have a very high vibration. The more of them you consume, the higher your energy and the greater your vitality. In turn, the higher your energy becomes, the more readily you can tap into your natural, God-given intuitive feelings. Thus, the more fruits and vegetables you enjoy, the easier it is for you to receive healing and insightful messages to help you take guided action when necessary.

It can sometimes seem hard to consume so many fresh fruits and vegetables every day. That's why we've been guided to enjoy natural juices and smoothies.

Juicing and Blending

There is a difference between juicing and blending, and we will talk about that in just a moment—but before we do, let's first look at the three main machines you could use to create a juice or smoothie:

— **Centrifugal juicer.** This is the most common type of juicer you will see in the marketplace. It has a very high spin speed. As you put the fruit or vegetable through the tunnel that feeds into the machine, a fast-spinning sieve chops up the food very, very finely, throwing solids into the bin while the juice is funneled out via a spigot. These are often the most inexpensive machines you can buy for this purpose and are a great way to start your juicing routine.

Many juicers now have openings large enough to fit an entire apple, so you don't have to chop up your fruits and vegetables into small pieces anymore. We do suggest, though, that you cut up apples and remove the seeds. The seeds actually contain small amounts of *cyanogenic glycosides,* and just as you might suspect from the name, these include trace amounts of cyanide. The occasional apple seed is not going to do significant damage, but it's best to reduce unnecessary risk as much as possible.

As the fast-moving metal mesh inside the machine separates the fiber component and the juice, it also creates a little heat that, theoretically, destroys some of the beneficial enzymes and nutrients inside the food. Now, this kind of juicing is far better than no juicing at all. If this is the only place you can begin, then please still go for it. Some companies report that their machines create very little heat, so it may not be a huge issue.

You can take the leftover fiber and pulp and scatter it out in the garden, in Mother Nature, and allow it to compost, becoming a natural fertilizer. You can also use the fiber to create healthy breads and muffins.

This type of juicer is wonderful for most fruits and vegetables, particularly those that are firm. When you use softer fruits and leafy green vegetables, however, many of the beneficial components get sifted into the rubbish section. To salvage the most juice out of soft produce, try this technique: Sandwich the soft fruit or leafy vegetables in between firmer vegetables. Roll up a leaf of kale and place it in between sticks of carrot. As you're gently pressing that through, you will be able to extract a little more juice from those leafy greens.

— **Masticating or cold-press juicer.** This is a much slower machine than the centrifugal juicer, which gives you juice in a matter of seconds. The cold-press juicer uses an auger. Think of it like a screw. You place small pieces of food into the feeder tube, which is often fairly small, so you'll have to spend some time cutting up your fruits and vegetables to fit. As you push your produce through the tube, the machine takes off bite-size pieces and then spirals them through a little tunnel. When the pieces get to the end, they get pressed up against a fine sieve until every last drop of juice is extracted. There are no fast-moving parts. There's no heat. The juice slowly drips out of the machine, and at the other end, the dry fiber component of the vegetable or fruit is removed.

This kind of juicer takes more time, but you do actually get more juice out of the fruits and vegetables. It is also excellent for leafy greens such as kale, spinach, and wheatgrass, as well as soft summer fruits such as mango, peach, and grapefruit. The cold-pressing ensures that no heat is used, which means that every enzyme and nutrient within that food is kept intact.

These machines are a little more expensive and take a bit of patience, but because no heat is involved, the juice lasts longer in the refrigerator. With the centrifugal juicer, you should probably aim to consume your juice within three to four hours. Cold-pressed juices keep for up to 24 hours in the right conditions. We like to enjoy our juices straightaway, and we encourage you to do the same. That way you can go back and create a new recipe the next time you feel like having a juice!

— **Blender.** Ordinary kitchen blenders are fine to use, but for silky-smooth smoothies, we prefer a high-powered machine such as the Vitamix. These machines are quite expensive, but are they ever powerful! The blades spin so fast that they break down the cell walls within the food. This means that the carrot you place into the blender (with a little bit of liquid—maybe some coconut water or organic apple juice) is pulverized once you switch the machine on high speed. It liquefies it. It opens up the cells so that the carrot is now exposing every piece of nutrition it has to offer, and your body can quickly and easily absorb it.

The big difference between juicing and blending is that the latter keeps all the fiber within the smoothie. If you place a carrot, some celery, and some kale into the blender with a bit of water and blend it up, you are drinking every part of those foods. If you put those same things through the juicer, you then throw away a good portion.

Juicing or blending is akin to drinking in the vibration and energy from the natural world. These beverages are easy to digest and are powerhouses of nutrition. Whether you are juicing or blending, you are outsourcing the act of chewing. If you think about the number of times you chew a mouthful of food, it's probably not very many. But when you blend or juice your fruits and vegetables, you are breaking them down to a degree to which you would never chew them.

Remember that these vegetables and fruits are making the ultimate sacrifice for us. When we eat a carrot, some leaves of kale, or a broccoli stalk, that plant can no longer live. We've removed it from the ground. We've ended that plant's life cycle. As we consume the life-force energy, we want to take in as much as we possibly can. That's why we love juices and smoothies—because the vibration of that plant is still so high. It's raw and pure.

In a simple juice or smoothie, you can drink in that life force. You can take that energy and vitality into your body and allow it to radiate within you. Every single one of your cells will be able to process what you've just consumed. Your digestive system will easily convert it into the high energy you've been craving. Since the ingredients are natural foods, your body instantly recognizes them.

When you enjoy regular juices and smoothies, you will find that you have a greater sense of clarity. These beverages clear away cloudiness within your mind and bring back an appreciation for simplicity in life.

As you rotate through different fruits and vegetables, you will find combinations that you like more than others. In this chapter, we share a few of our favorites.

Heart-Opening Smoothie Greens

When you create any kind of juice or smoothie, you are going to be receiving healing benefits. But when you focus on beautiful, lush, vibrant greens such as spinach, kale, celery, cucumber, and lettuce, you are connecting to the heart-healing energy of emerald-green light. And *who else* is connected to emerald-green energy? None other than the powerful angelic healer Archangel Raphael!

The green energy allows our hearts to open and expand, bringing with it a compassion for humanity. When we look out upon the world, we see opportunities to help and heal. We don't focus selfishly on personal gain. Instead, our primary focus is on us as members of a greater community: *How may we serve? How may we help?* As our hearts open, we recognize that it is no longer just about us. It's about *all of us* connecting together.

Green smoothies look far more frightening than they really are. We encourage you to try your own. A green drink might initially look uninviting in color but can taste delicious! Add some kale to your favorite juice or a green apple and kiwi to the next smoothie you make.

There are several green foods that are particularly wonderful to open up and awaken your intuition:

Chlorella

Chlorella is a superfood that you can find at the health-food store. Given that this algae is a little more challenging for your body to break down and digest, we suggest getting open-cell or cracked-cell chlorella, where the nutrients are more accessible for you to absorb.

Chlorella is excellent at detoxing heavy metals and has been shown to protect against toxicity from mercury, lead, cadmium, copper, polychlorinated biphenyls (PCBs), dioxins, and uranium. Following the Chernobyl nuclear disaster, for example, chlorella was used to help many people who were exposed to radiation.

Chlorella helps remove negative influences from your life—quite often, people who aren't serving your highest good. If there are those around you who always seem to attract drama, they are only slowing you down. These people many times don't have a desire to change. They enjoy the drama and thrive on it.

Trying to help people like this is very challenging. They proclaim that they long for peace yet are unwilling to take even the simplest of suggestions. If you feel guided, extend your offer of help and then let go of *their* choices. They know where to find you if they want your assistance, but please don't delay your joy any longer by expending your efforts in an uphill battle.

When you take chlorella, it clears your path of these unhealthy distractions in a peaceful, healing way. Everyone involved feels comfortable and secure with the gentle transition.

Kale

Kale is so beautifully nutritious that it's considered a superfood, as we discussed in Chapter 5. When you consume it as a juice or smoothie, you are breaking open every last drop of healing it has to give. You enjoy all the benefits it offers physically and energetically.

The energy that surrounds kale is uplifting and heart opening. By including this food in your smoothies, you're giving yourself a natural multivitamin! Start off by adding a small handful of fresh, organic kale. Then, over time, increase the amount to your liking. Kale is a detoxing food as well, so if you go too quickly, you may cleanse faster than you'd like. For a gentle yet powerful cleanse, begin slowly and work your way up.

Spirulina

Spirulina is a potent green that you can purchase at your local health-food store. We love Hawaiian spirulina in particular, because the oceans in Hawaii are very clean and filled with natural minerals. So when the spirulina is harvested in this seawater, it absorbs all the minerals present—many more than when grown in ordinary saltwater. Both kinds of spirulina are going to be healing and beneficial, yet the Hawaiian spirulina is *supercharged* with nutrition.

The emerald-green color resonates with Archangel Raphael. By enjoying spirulina, you're giving your healing angels permission to help you. Remember that your angels are bound by the Law of Free Will, so they are unable to act on your behalf until you call upon their Divine assistance. Your angels *can* intervene when you're working with crystals or flowers, for example, or consuming certain foods.

Spirulina brings your angels closer to you, thereby making it easier to hear their messages. You'll find that your meditations are deeper and more healing when you start adding it to your diet.

Spirulina contains over 100 nutrients, which makes it one of the most complete supplements available. Scientific studies have shown that naturally occurring vitamins are often much more effective than synthetic ones. Spirulina is easily absorbed by your body and nourishes you with B vitamins, iron, fatty acids, *and* protein. It also contains vitamin A, a powerful antioxidant, preventing damage to your cells.

You can buy spirulina as a powder, tablets, or even capsules. We like to spoon the powder into our smoothies and juices. Just by adding a teaspoon to your glass of fresh, organic apple juice, you will start to notice the benefits. Instantly, you'll be able to sense the green energy.

Because it is so wonderfully cleansing, you may feel guided to start at a lower dose. Begin with a half teaspoon and slowly increase to a teaspoon—which equates to roughly 3,000 mg—three times per day. Most spirulina tablets are 500 mg, so you may be taking six at a time if you choose this form.

Spiritual-Smoothie Superfoods

Acai

The acai berry comes from a palm tree in the Amazon rain forest. Highly nutritious, it's rumored to have sustained Amazonian tribes when they were threatened with starvation. In Brazil it's commonly called "Beauty Berry," because it contains so many uplifting, youth-enhancing properties. When you take acai, you feel young at heart. Its powerful antioxidant properties combat the effects of aging. It has hundreds of times the antioxidants compared with the majority of everyday fruits.

Acai contains a combination of essential fatty acids—omega-3, omega-6, and omega-9—that can help enhance your natural beauty. It brings shine and strength to your hair, and smoothness and a radiant glow to your skin.

Acai has most of the nutrients commonly present in fruits and vegetables. However, it also contains many other special and unique phytonutrients. Research suggests that there are between 50 and 75 unidentified natural compounds not found in any other food. These mysterious compounds may be responsible for its highly nourishing quality.

In naturopathic philosophy, we say that the whole is greater than the sum of its parts. This basically means that if we alter the perfect design of nature by extracting just one of the natural compounds, it may not work as expected. The best example of this is aspirin (acetylsalicylic acid), derived from salicin, which comes from white willow bark. When given as a whole extract, this herb heals pain and inflammation. So, the assumption was made that taking out one of its active compounds would lead to a more concentrated effect. Unfortunately, there is no replacement for God's creation. The synthetic version can cause stomach issues, whereas the complete extract can *heal* stomach problems. So while we may not yet fully understand all the constituents of acai, we can trust that God has created harmony within this nourishing plant.

Most preparations of acai are freeze-dried berries that you can purchase as capsules or powder. You can add one to three tablespoons of the powder to your favorite smoothie. It is also available as frozen puree. There are prepared juices available; however, many contain only small amounts of acai and are often laden with added sugars.

Through ethical harvesting, several companies are providing a sustainable future for Amazonian locals. Previously, for every ton of berry powder, there could be 20 tons of discarded seeds. Instead of being thrown away, the seeds are now being used by locals in place of firewood. This alternative to timber even helps lessen the deforestation of the Amazon.

The purple color brings through a strong and protective energy. Acai is connected to Archangel Michael, who is associated with courage, strength, and purification. Thus, it shields you from harsh situations and psychic attack. With the support of Archangel Michael, the berry helps you uncover your true life's purpose. If you wonder what you are meant to be doing, try some acai. It shines a light on new opportunities.

Acai helps you clear negative thoughts and transform them into love. When you focus on love, you realize that anything is possible and begin to attract miracles. Acai encourages you to never give up, as the miracle may be just around the corner. Keep persisting and know that you are being safeguarded from negativity as you fearlessly move ahead. Acai resonates with the third-eye chakra and enhances your gifts of clairvoyance.

When you take acai, you'll learn that changing your mind doesn't have to be a bad thing. Maybe in the past you committed to something but have now lost your passion for it. If you've tried to reignite that spark, to no avail, it may be time to move on, and acai will ease the transition.

Camu Camu

Camu camu is a small fruit also found in the Amazon rain forest and traditionally used by the people of Peru. It has one of the highest concentrations of natural vitamin C of any food. Just one teaspoon of camu camu powder gives you an abundance—more than you would get if you ate ten oranges! It's also filled with many other vitamins and minerals to sustain a healthy body.

Traditionally, camu camu was consumed to boost the immune system and fight viral infections. This, indeed, would have been a perfect application, given the high concentration of vitamin C. It's also been used to strengthen the nervous system and enhance mental performance.

Take one teaspoon of powder per day. You can simply mix it with a glass of water or add it to your smoothie. The taste is sour, so make sure it will go with the flavors of your juice before you ruin a whole batch!

Camu camu can be wonderfully helpful to highly sensitive people. If you're empathetic—you feel other people's emotions and pain—it helps you identify what is your "stuff" and what is others'. If you get overwhelmed and anxious around large groups of people, consider taking a dose of camu camu. It shields your aura, lending you a feeling of safety. It appears to create a bubble around you where others can no longer invade your personal space. Taking camu camu can be helpful before you attend a spiritual expo or festival. While these are great places to be introduced to wonderful souls, new therapies, and beautiful crystals, there are also going to be jealous and competitive people present. Being sensitive to those harsh vibrations may put a damper on your experience. The auric shielding that takes place when you enjoy camu camu helps you stay secure by warding off psychic attack.

Due to camu camu's healing qualities, it also helps you attract the perfect healer or teacher. You'll be met with synchronistic encounters that will lead you to the best people who will support you right now.

Coconut Water

Coconut water is the nourishing liquid from the inside of a fresh young coconut. It's a natural source of electrolytes, which help hydrate the body. If you don't have a good balance of electrolytes, you may be dehydrated even if you're drinking eight glasses of water per day! Electrolytes are lost during physical exertion and times of stress.

I (Robert) learned the importance of electrolytes firsthand. I enjoy going to the gym and doing group fitness classes. When I participate in a spin or aerobics class, I challenge myself more than when I exercise on my own. I feel as if I have to keep up with the rest of the class—or even do harder options. A couple of years ago, after a few of my workouts, I felt really drained and just "off."

I began having muscle spasms and ended up in the hospital emergency room. The staff ran all kinds of tests, looking for signs of infection or some other explanation. They weren't able to find anything, so they sent me home.

A couple of weeks later, the same thing happened: I was unhappily back in the ER with uncontrollable—and uncomfortable—muscle spasms. Again, they found nothing that could be causing this kind of reaction except that my electrolytes were a little unbalanced.

That was all I needed to hear. I immediately came up with a treatment plan for myself to ensure that the spasms wouldn't recur. When sweating during exercise, you lose electrolytes. That's what most sports drinks contain (along with artificial sweeteners, artificial colors, and who knows what other toxins). So I started using coconut water in my smoothies. It was a simple change, and initially I was doubtful that it would solve the problem. But now I have a glass of coconut water (either by itself or as part of my smoothie) every day, and those muscle spasms have never returned! It's been over two years, and I can now exercise even harder. I don't feel exhausted afterward; instead, I feel recharged!

Energetically, coconut water allows all the components of your body to talk to one another. It's wonderful if you've felt stuck or lacked motivation. The coconut shows you that your body is capable of fulfilling all your desires; it just needs a little fine-tuning. Clairvoyantly, you can see the coconut water creating an electric charge throughout your physical being. It inspires your cells to reach their utmost potential, which in turn allows *you* to accomplish tasks with great speed.

Goji Berries

Goji berries have been used for thousands of years in traditional Chinese medicine. They are said to boost the *chi,* or life force, of whoever consumes them. These nutritive berries promote longevity. There are tales of monks consuming goji berries (as well as other tonic herbs) who lived well over 100 years. They contain 18 amino acids—including 8 essential amino acids, which are the ones our bodies cannot make.

The dried berries can be eaten as a snack and added to your own trail-mix blend. Please be aware that the source is highly important. As you consume superfoods to strengthen your intuition and build a closer relationship with God and your angels, you want the best product you can find. Most goji berries come from China, which has a very different organic certification process from that in the West. Certified-organic products in China can still contain toxic chemicals. The location, water quality, and soil often are not taken into account and may be filled with harmful compounds. Please only purchase certified-organic goji berries from a reputable source.

Goji berries expand your energy. They help you feel enlivened and motivated. On the one hand, they excite you, giving you a feeling of drive . . . yet on the other, they encourage you to take your time and work peacefully. Think of highly productive Buddhist monks: They are industrious but don't allow themselves to become flustered, stressed, or rushed. This is how the goji berries encourage *you* to work.

They also help activate your own energetic-healing abilities. We are all blessed with the capacity to bring through healing vibrations. Whether you do so through prayer or other modalities, goji berries can accentuate your gifts.

Maca

Maca is a superfood of the Incas that naturally grows between 9,000 and 14,000 feet above sea level. Its ability to thrive in such extreme environments identify it as full of resilient, healing properties. Maca helps you cope with stress physically and mentally. It contains numerous compounds that promote a sense of well-being and comfort. It allows your body and mind to adapt to the situations you're in, giving you greater energy and clarity.

Maca has a unique set of plant compounds that stimulates your hypothalamus and pituitary gland—which can have a balancing effect on your metabolism and hormones. Traditionally it has been used to support menopause, boost the immune system, and promote vitality.

Maca helps you clear away negative energies. Its wonderful cleansing action heals you emotionally and energetically. Holding on to unforgiveness, anger, and resentment serves no purpose. These lower emotions are only harming you. With the help of maca, you can willingly release them . . . in exchange for comfort. You'll come to realize that negative energy (in any form) is only taking up space that could be better utilized by love. Maca helps you trust that all is well.

Take one to four teaspoons per day mixed into a glass of water or juice. There are two types available: *raw* and *gelatinized.* Many people report that the gelatinized (or cooked) maca is much easier on their stomachs. It is more digestible, as the long-chain starches have already been broken down. The traditional way of consuming maca in Peru has always been to cook it first.

Maqui

Maqui is another strong antioxidant, this time coming from southern Chile. Traditionally, the juice of the berries was used to bring strength and stamina. Take one teaspoon of powder mixed with water or juice for a potent remedy. The free-radical-fighting power of maqui slows the aging process, helps your cardiovascular system, and keeps you healthy overall.

Maqui supports you in feeling that anything is possible. Despite what other people may have said, *you* have the power within you to accomplish amazing things. Give yourself permission to follow your dreams and know that it's only a matter of time before you achieve them.

As we've taken this journey through various smoothie superfoods, you may have noticed that a great deal of them possess antioxidant properties. So, unsurprisingly, if you enjoy a range of fresh, natural foods, you'll be consuming a diet rich in antioxidants!

Every nutrient has its own vibration. Intuitively, when you have *more* antioxidants, you are even more protected from harsh energies. This allows you to stay open to your God-given abilities and remain unaffected by negativity.

Nourishing Additions to Your Smoothies

To give your smoothies an extra layer of nutrition and decadence, a couple of teaspoons of organic nut butter adds a delicious richness. Where possible, use raw nut butters, but the occasional roasted nut butter is a tasty treat.

Use our nut mylks from the previous chapter as nourishing bases for your smoothie recipes in place of apple juice, coconut water, or water. You'll get all the wonderful healing qualities, as well as great flavor! You can also just add a small handful of nuts to your smoothie, and provided that your blender is strong enough, it will pulverize them into liquid.

Spiritual Chakra Smoothies

We've created healing smoothies that focus on each of the seven major chakras, plus the ear and hand chakras. These spiritual smoothies are simple to make and taste great! As you enjoy them, the energies from the different ingredients will help awaken your intuitive gifts.

These smoothies are mostly fruit based, as fresh fruit has such a high vibration. You can certainly include more vegetable components; just be aware that doing so will change both the taste and color. We adore green smoothies and would happily encourage you to add kale, spinach, romaine lettuce, chard, and other leafy greens to any of these recipes.

Trust your personal intuition with these psychic smoothies, and feel free to adjust quantities or ingredients to better suit you. It doesn't matter if you remove an ingredient or add a new one; the important thing is to ensure you're *enjoying* these highly nourishing and uplifting drinks!

Simply put all the ingredients into your blender at once and blend. If your blender has variable speeds, begin with a slow setting for a few seconds, then increase to high. Allow everything to blend for around one minute to give you a smooth-textured drink. If you're finding that the result is not as smooth as you'd like, you may want to look into purchasing a more powerful machine.

CROWN

10 saffron threads (soak in ¼ cup boiling water for 10 minutes)
¼ cup raw macadamia nuts
¼ cup raw sunflower seeds (hulled)
1 banana
1 pear (core removed)
3 cups organic apple juice

THIRD EYE

1 cup blueberries
1 tbsp. acai powder (soak in ¼ cup filtered, non-fluoridated water for 10 minutes)
1 cup pineapple
3 cups coconut water

EAR

Seeds from 1 pomegranate
½ cup grapes
2 cups organic apple juice

THROAT

1 cup cooled thyme tea (see next chapter for more information on teas)
2 cups Cashew Mylk (recipe on page 90)
¼ cup blueberries

HEART

2 cups kale (stems removed)
1 tsp. spirulina
1 cup sliced cucumber
1 stalk celery
4 cups organic apple juice

SOLAR PLEXUS

½ lemon with skin
1 cup pineapple
½ cup mango
3 cups coconut water

SACRAL

1 orange
1-inch piece of turmeric
½ cup cantaloupe
½ cup papaya
1 carrot
2 cups water

ROOT

1 cup strawberries
½ cup raspberries
¼ cup fresh beets (skin removed)
½ cup watermelon
4 cups coconut water

HAND

1-inch piece of fresh ginger
2 sprigs fresh mint
½ cup mango
1 cup kale
3 cups coconut water

Think of these juices and smoothies as your medicine. This is your supplement, your multivitamin—the drink through which you will receive the elixir of life. And if you want to enrich your diet with additional vitamins and minerals, the Appendix lists both the physical and spiritual properties of common nutritional supplements.

As you enjoy vibrant nutrition, your energy will be uplifted. Your intuition will switch back on because the vibration of nature, as a beneficial side effect, takes your life to a higher level.

In the next chapter, we will share with you the healing power of teas and herbal medicines.

CHAPTER EIGHT

Herbal Teas and Medicines for Intuition

For centuries people have been looking into their teacups to find answers in the tea leaves. These brews have always held a spiritual energy. When you take time to make yourself a soothing cup of herbal tea, you are allowing yourself to go within. You soften your thoughts and begin to hear the voice of your intuition.

In herbal medicine, infusions are powerful healing teas that treat a wide variety of ailments. They have long been used as simple remedies that could be made at home. A good cup of peppermint tea can do wonders for an upset stomach, and a brew of chamomile can relax your anxieties and stress levels.

The Art of Making Tea

In our current convenience-focused age, many just grab a tea bag and pop it into a cup of hot water. This instant tea is really just flavored water. If you want to gain all the spiritual benefits that a healing infusion has to offer, you need to take some *time* in preparing it.

Tea is best made in a closed vessel—either a teapot or a cup with a small saucer placed on top to serve as a lid. When you brew tea this way, you allow the beautiful aromatic qualities to recirculate back into the liquid. You know that uplifting fragrance emanating from peppermint tea? Well, that represents most of the healing oils floating off into the atmosphere. If you brew it in a teapot or cup with a lid, the steam condenses back into the infusion.

For most herbal teas, you'll want to brew it for at least five minutes in boiling water. You can allow your tea to brew longer and get an even more potent infusion. A general rule is one teaspoon of herb per cup of water, plus one extra for the teapot. So if your teapot holds two cups of water, you would add three teaspoons of herb.

Purchase organic loose herbs so you can create your own magical blends to suit your tastes and needs. You'll want to store them in airtight containers and out of direct sunlight so they retain their potency. When customizing your infusion, consider which of the following herbs may fit your spiritual needs.

Spiritual Properties of Various Teas

Calendula is strongly connected with Archangel Raphael. This means that the tea will *bring* healing as well as *activate* your innate healing abilities. When you drink calendula, you stand tall as a powerful healer. This tea repairs your aura and brings energetic protection.

Chamomile helps attract abundance. It relaxes your energy, which allows you to become receptive. The Universe and God always have your best interests in mind. When things seem challenging, it can be for one of two reasons: You are trying to go in a different direction than where you are truly being guided, or you are unwilling to receive help and support along the way. When you drink chamomile, you let down your guard and *let in* the healing love of God and your angels.

Fennel tea (made from the seeds) can help reduce sugar cravings. On an energetic level it gives you a "pat on the back." As a healer or reader, you may focus on helping others rather than devoting time to yourself. By drinking this infusion, you remember that it's okay to have a rest every now and then. You can relax, take a day off, and just enjoy life.

Ginger tea releases anger and frustration. It helps you let go of resentment and jealousy, bringing you to a place of contentment and balance.

Hibiscus tea makes a wonderful ruby-colored infusion. It allows you to accept your sensitive side. Know that being sensitive isn't a weakness; it's an asset! By picking up on the subtle energies around you, you will know much more easily when you should move on. The hibiscus brings you and your loved ones together. It heals past wounds and promotes forgiveness.

Lavender relaxes your mind and quiets the ego voice. It is beautiful before a meditation, as it resonates with the third-eye chakra— your center of clairvoyance. This summons psychic visions and intuitive insights. Lavender brings a deeper spiritual understanding. This herb is connected with Archangel Michael, who helps cast away any fears about embracing your spiritual gifts.

Lemongrass wards off distractions and procrastination. If you are struggling to get something done and finding many excuses not to do it, then you need lemongrass tea! It brings you clarity of purpose so you can get to work. It also shows you the tremendous benefit that completing this task will serve both you and others. Lemongrass sharpens your focus and stops people from interrupting your important job.

Nettle tea is great for when you feel worn-out and drained. It is a highly nutritious infusion that supports your body physically. It provides energetic protection, giving you time to recharge. As your body and mind reset, you learn new ways to handle situations. Understand the lessons involved in your current situation and you won't have to repeat them.

Peppermint helps motivate and inspire you, bringing you new creative ideas on how to achieve your dreams. It clears and balances the sacral and solar-plexus chakras, lending you confidence and self-esteem.

Rose tea opens your heart. It attracts compassion; understanding; healing; and, of course, love. When drinking this tea, you become very aware of your language. Every word you speak will have the essence of love attached to it. All your communications will be uplifting and centered around healing. You'll find that you have no time for gossip or negativity. Instead, you will become an inspiration to those around you—who will wonder why you are so peaceful and then will want to join you on that path of tranquility.

Rosemary may not be an herb you'd commonly think of for tea. It tastes exactly like you'd expect, but the energy is beautiful! Rosemary has an affinity for the head area. It clears away unwanted thoughts, lifts negative thinking in favor of a positive attitude, and assists with concentration. Rosemary resonates with the third-eye chakra and releases pressure surrounding your spiritual path. Allow yourself to enjoy this wonderful journey, and don't put unnecessary deadlines in place.

Saffron tea sounds so indulgent and somewhat royal. And saffron *is* the most expensive herb in the world. Thankfully, you only need the smallest amount to make a very powerful tea. Add five to ten good-quality saffron threads (parts of the pistil of a crocus) to a cup of boiling water. Allow to steep for a minimum of ten minutes so the saffron can fully give itself to the water. Research trials have shown that saffron helps ease symptoms of premenstrual syndrome and feelings of depression. Spiritually, saffron is associated with Archangel Raziel, the spiritual-teacher angel, and unlocks the mysteries of the Universe, allowing you to learn deep, esoteric concepts. It awakens and clears all your energy centers and connects you to God.

Thyme is another herb you might not have considered brewing. This tea opens up your centers of communication and resonates with the throat chakra to help you speak and write with passion and purpose. If you're finding it difficult to express yourself, try thyme tea.

How to Take Herbal Medicines

As a sensitive and spiritual person, you may not need high doses of herbal supplements, as your body is receptive to these healing compounds and will immediately begin to utilize them. Where it may take others three to four weeks to observe a change, you might see improvements in just a matter of days. The reason you were guided to read this book is because you are an intuitive person. You understand that what you eat changes your entire energy. You've noticed that you can't handle certain foods or drinks because they just don't agree with your delicate body. So, before you dive into high doses of herbs, check in with your intuitive feelings.

Herbal medicines come in a variety of forms, including tablets, capsules, teas, liquid extracts, and tinctures. Whichever form you choose, please ensure it's sourced from a reliable company, sustainably harvested, and organic or wild-crafted. This will give you the best results, as well as the highest energy.

Any form of herb will have a healing influence, yet there is something especially powerful about a liquid. When you take a tincture, it brings through the energy and vibration of the plant. Add the appropriate dose to a small glass of water. The amount of water isn't important as long as you drink the entirety. I (Robert) prefer to take my herbs in a full glass of water. This way, the taste, as well as any alcohol that may be used in the extract, is more diluted. With the exception of gymnema, we don't advise that you take the herbal tinctures "neat," or undiluted.

If you are on any other medications or have preexisting health concerns, please always check with your health-care practitioner before starting any herbal medicines.

Herbs for Endocrine Health

Bacopa (*Bacopa monnieri*) helps you cope with stress and organize your thoughts. I (Robert) often think of this as the perfect herbal medicine for accountants. Visualize yourself with piles of tasks you need to complete, each one requiring intense concentration. You need to get everything done, but you don't want to burn the candle at both ends.

This is where bacopa comes in to boost focus, clarity, and memory. It's the perfect exam herb! It heals anxiety and exhaustion. Bacopa may have a thyroid-healing function and help stimulate thyroid hormones, too.

Take 30 drops of tincture twice per day to help your thyroid and boost your brainpower.

Black cohosh (*Cimicifuga racemosa*) is an estrogen-regulating herb that also helps balance the pituitary gland, hypothalamus, and ovarian glands. It inhibits the production of luteinizing hormone, which comes from the pituitary. It's thought that surges of luteinizing hormone are responsible for hot flashes. This is why black cohosh is frequently used by menopausal women.

In the past, fears were raised that black cohosh might cause liver disturbances and potentially be linked to cancer. One of the original studies that highlighted this concern was later discredited. The product tested, it was found, didn't even contain black cohosh; rather, a known cancer-causing agent was substituted.

Since then a number of studies have been conducted to assess black cohosh and its safety. Researchers suggest that black cohosh regulates estrogen production, depending on dose. If you use a small amount of the herb, it will regulate; high amounts will overwhelm.

Take 20 drops of tincture twice per day to help balance and regulate your body's hormones.

Bladderwrack (*Fucus vesiculosus*), better known as kelp, is a key herb for the thyroid. It is filled with minerals, especially iodine, which stimulates thyroid-gland function. This boosts your metabolism and can assist with losing stubborn weight.

Try 20 drops of tincture twice a day to give your thyroid gland the nourishment it needs.

Bugleweed (*Lycopus spp.*) is used when too much thyroid hormone is being produced. It lowers thyroid function by slowing the production of thyroid-stimulating hormone.

If you have an overactive thyroid, it's always best to seek treatment with a qualified professional and consult with him or her on dosages.

Chaste tree (*Vitex agnus-castus*) is commonly given to women to balance female hormones. It's prescribed for premenstrual symptoms, as well as a range of cycle-related issues. That being said, it also has a beneficial effect on men. It can subdue a fiery temper by calibrating hormones. It also regulates the hypothalamus and ovarian glands, promoting overall balance.

Chaste tree helps balance the pituitary gland and may work in cases where the pituitary hormones are too weak or too strong. It is wonderful for lactating mothers because it helps the pituitary gland produce prolactin, which stimulates the flow of breast milk. However, it also *slows down* the production of prolactin when necessary. This is the beauty of natural medicine; the innate intelligence of the herb can determine what actions you need right now.

Take 20 drops of tincture twice per day to balance hormones and regulate the menstrual cycle.

Coleus (*Coleus forskohlii*) is a key herb for easing metabolic syndrome—characterized by fatigue, weight gain, and blood-sugar fluctuations. It stimulates the thyroid gland and boosts metabolism. It works harmoniously with the hypothalamus, pituitary, and adrenal glands, also.

Coleus stimulates many of your endocrine glands, which is why it has such a profound effect on tired, overweight, debilitated individuals. It is thought that the herb moves fat cells out of storage so the body can use them as energy. Fat is a more abundant source of energy than carbohydrates or protein, so when stored fat is burned off as fuel, you feel recharged and motivated.

Try 20 drops of tincture three times per day to give your body the reset it may need.

Echinacea (*Echinacea spp.*) is commonly used to treat colds and flu. However, this herb is a powerful immune stimulant, which means it is best used in the very early stages of infection. It's perfect to take for immune support when others around you are sick.

There are several different types of echinacea, and each appears to have immune-boosting properties. The most effective are *Echinacea angustifolia* and *Echinacea purpurea.* Some products contain another form, *Echinacea pallida,* which has fewer healing properties compared with the other two species.

Echinacea stimulates the production of white blood cells, which mount your immune response. It may operate by balancing the thymus gland, which controls these actions.

Take 25 drops of tincture three to four times per day to protect yourself against infection, or 10 drops twice daily for a gentle cleanse and immune-system regulation.

False unicorn root (*Chamaelirium luteum*) has such a magical name that it must have equally magical properties! Indeed, it is a highly effective fertility herb that regulates estrogen levels and balances the hypothalamus, pituitary, and ovarian glands. I (Robert) have seen false unicorn root create miracles for patients. Women who were trying to conceive for years became pregnant after only a short time on a regimen with this herb.

At one point, false unicorn root was nearing endangerment, as it was being overharvested in the wild. Cultivation of the herb proved difficult and is only recently being done successfully. Because of this, the price of false unicorn root is quite high. Please ensure that you purchase your herb ethically and sustainably.

Take 8 drops of tincture twice daily to enhance your fertility.

Fenugreek (*Trigonella foenum-graecum*) is a nutritive and cleansing herb. It helps to lower blood-sugar levels, and so may have a beneficial effect on the pancreas. It also stimulates the flow of breast milk in lactating mothers, which suggests a possible influence on the pituitary gland.

Take 15 drops of tincture three times per day just prior to meals.

Gotu kola (*Centella asiatica*) supports the nervous system and is said to stimulate the pineal gland. Traditionally, it has been used as a rejuvenator that helps activate the mind. It has a nourishing quality that brings new energy to a clouded and foggy head, relaxes your nerves, and helps you better cope with stress. Gotu kola may also have an influence on the pituitary gland.

There are ancient stories of people taking this herb daily and reaching ages of over 200 years. Some older sources of information about gotu kola can be misleading, as it was commonly referred to as *brahmi,* as was the herb bacopa. Since the two plants were called the same name, a lot of these references may be conflicting.

Take 20 drops of tincture two or three times per day to gain clarity and vitality.

Gymnema (*Gymnema sylvestre*) regulates blood sugar and heals the pancreas. The liquid tincture blocks the receptors for sweetness on your tongue, changing the way you taste sugary foods. The effect is instantaneous, and after a few weeks you'll find your appetite for certain foods naturally changes.

Scientific studies performed on gymnema found that it may heal and restore the pancreas. They tested patients with a poorly functioning pancreas (resulting in high blood-sugar levels) and discovered that the herb stimulated the pancreas to start working better. Insulin also lowers the levels of sugar in your blood, but doesn't heal the pancreas. That's what makes this herb so special.

Put 10 drops of tincture directly on the tongue 15 minutes before eating, three times per day.

Lemon balm (*Melissa officinalis*) is a calming and relaxing herb. It reduces anxiety and lifts thoughts of depression. It also heals an upset stomach, which makes it perfect for nervous butterflies.

Take 12 drops of tincture three times per day. You may also find adding 4 drops to your water bottle beneficial to help you stay calm all day long.

Lemon balm can slightly reduce the action of the thyroid gland, so it may be useful in hyperthyroidism. If you have an overactive thyroid, it's always best to coordinate treatment with a qualified professional.

Licorice (*Glycyrrhiza glabra*) is one of a handful of herbal medicines that have an agreeable taste. It contains *glycyrrhizin,* which is 50 to 100 times sweeter than sucrose.

Licorice is a powerful herb with many notable actions, including anti-inflammatory, energizing, hormone balancing, stress reducing, and expectorant, which is often the reason people self-prescribe it. However, this respected herb also has a steroidal action. It can raise your body's levels of cortisone, which is very healing when needed, yet may cause issues if you take licorice for lengthy periods of time (over three months). In large doses, licorice may also raise blood pressure, so those with high blood pressure should avoid taking it.

Licorice balances the hypothalamus, pituitary, and adrenal glands. It restores your adrenal function and is excellent in cases of exhaustion and fatigue. It slows the breakdown of adrenal hormones, which means that you have more sustained energy. This gives your body time to naturally repair and restore itself.

Enjoy 15 tasty drops of licorice extract two to three times per day.

Oregano oil (*Origanum vulgare*) is a powerful antimicrobial. Some suggest that the pineal gland can become clogged with calcium, thereby blocking your spiritual gifts. The theory holds that nanobacteria (extremely small bacterial organisms) lodge themselves in the pineal gland and shield themselves within a calcium shell. Regular antibiotic treatments can't break through the tough calcium exterior—but oregano oil can. It penetrates and dissolves the calcium shells and removes the bacteria.

As with all concentrated oils, you must be cautious with the dosage. People over the age of 18 may be able to take commercial oregano-oil capsules. Alternatively, you can add a few drops to a diffuser and allow the aroma to spread through your home.

Peony (*Paeonia lactiflora*) can balance the ratio between luteinizing hormone and follicle-stimulating hormone, two hormones in women produced by the pituitary gland. Peony normalizes estrogen levels by helping regulate the pituitary gland.

When peony is combined with licorice, it creates a synergistic effect that research has shown can balance the hypothalamus, pituitary gland, and ovaries. This benefits conditions like polycystic ovarian syndrome (PCOS) or cases when male hormones are too high in women.

When you take 15 drops of tincture twice per day, you allow your hormones to be regulated.

Rehmannia (*Rehmannia glutinosa*) reduces inflammation and restores energy, stimulating the adrenal glands in a nourishing and healing way. It is one of only a handful of herbs (licorice is another) that repairs the adrenals. Rehmannia also helps you cope with stress and find a new way of handling your current situation.

Take 20 drops of tincture twice daily for adrenal healing and repair.

Saint-John's-wort (*Hypericum perforatum*) is well known as an herb that curtails depressive thoughts and helps you find joy. When you take Saint-John's-wort, it feels like a cloud has been lifted from you. Things become clearer, and you start to smile again.

This herb supports your body in the production of serotonin. Your body naturally manufactures this feel-good hormone; however, during times of depression, you may become serotonin deficient. Saint-John's-wort allows your brain to gain more benefit from the serotonin you currently have, while also helping produce more. Serotonin is then converted into melatonin, the hormone needed to balance your sleep/wake cycle and to cope with time-zone changes.

This transformation happens within the pineal gland. Having adequate serotonin means that you can convert good amounts of melatonin and enjoy a healthy sleep pattern. It is also thought by some that melatonin production is stimulated by moonlight. So spending 15 minutes in the moonlight may help, too.

Take 20 drops of Saint-John's-wort tincture before bed to help create fuel for your pineal gland, as well as balance the hypothalamus and the adrenal glands.

(*Please note that Saint-John's-wort also stimulates the liver and may interact with other medications.*)

Sarsaparilla (*Smilax spp.*) is a cleansing herb that has more of an affinity for men. It removes toxins and stimulates male hormones. Given this effect, it may exert an influence on the testes.

Take 15 drops of tincture twice daily for a gentle cleanse.

Saw palmetto (*Serenoa repens*) is a male tonic that balances the prostate and testes. It's often used in cases of benign prostatic hyperplasia (BPH) but can also bring healing for men in general. It may influence the adrenal glands and support feelings of energy and motivation.

All forms of saw palmetto are nourishing, but liposterolic extracts (those containing fatty acids) may have a more powerful effect.

Take 10 drops of tincture three times per day to balance male hormones.

Siberian ginseng (*Eleutherococcus senticosus*) is excellent for people who are tired and drained. When you feel like you are running on empty, this herb can help. It gives you a natural source of energy and helps you cope with any stress. Part of this action may be due to its positive influence on the adrenal glands. It also helps the thyroid gland and may have a slight effect on the pancreas, as it balances blood sugar.

Take 30 drops of tincture twice daily to restore your body's natural energy reserves.

Herbs to Support Your Hand Chakras

There are a number of herbal medicines that can help stimulate the eccrine glands and your hand chakras in a supportive way. Don't worry—taking these herbs won't mean you'll suddenly be dripping in sweat. The wisdom of nature connects with your body and determines what healing you need right now. If your sweat glands are blocked or sluggish, these herbs can help stimulate and awaken them. If they're fine, the herbs nourish and support you more generally.

For the best effect, these herbs should be taken as a hot tea. Brewing them in a teapot allows all their medicinal qualities to combine with the water. Let your infusion sit for ten minutes before pouring into your favorite cup and enjoying. Sip the tea while still warm, as this helps the healing energy of the herbs spread through your body. Remember to brew your tea in a closed vessel; if you just use a tea bag in a cup, some of the therapeutic benefit can be lost in the steam.

Cayenne (*Capsicum annuum*) is a very strong, warming herb. It stimulates your metabolism, which can assist with weight loss. When you eat foods that include cayenne, you will start to feel hotter. You might get flushed, as the cayenne boosts your circulation. The heat from the herb opens up your sweat glands and allows you to perspire.

You only need the smallest amount of cayenne to feel its heat. Add a pinch of powder to a pot of hot water, and allow it to steep. Before you pour yourself a cup, taste a teaspoonful first to ensure it isn't too spicy, and dilute with water if necessary.

Elder (*Sambucus nigra*) is available in two forms—the berry and the flower. Elderberry is an excellent antiviral. A number of scientific studies have shown how elderberry extracts are able to inhibit the replication of a range of viruses. For best results, look for powdered-capsule or tablet products, as the liquid extracts don't hold on to their antiviral property for very long. In this case, though, we are more interested in the elder flowers, as they help promote sweating.

The elder tree has a long history connected to ancient mysticism. Even farmers would refer to the spirit of this tree as the "Elder Mother." This herb has a powerful energy that awakens your intuition and opens your chakras. Elder flowers have a connection to the head and are excellent for people with constant colds, runny noses, or hay fever.

Ginger (*Zingiber officinale*) is a warming herb that stimulates your circulation. As your blood spreads through the superficial layers of your skin, it clears the eccrine glands. The ginger carries with it the nutrition that's available to your body. Think of it like a courier transporting your vitamins and minerals to the locations that need them most.

Along with this nutrition, your energy also flows through the same path. According to traditional Chinese medicine, the blood and energy/vital force follow one another. So if your circulation is stimulated, so too is your energy, and therefore your intuition.

Ginkgo (*Ginkgo biloba*) is another herb that may help sweating through circulation, but in a non-heating way. Ginkgo is one of a few herbs that has what's known as anti–platelet activating factor (anti-PAF). This means that ginkgo prevents your blood from becoming too thick, allowing for easy circulation. This property may be one of the reasons ginkgo is able to help your blood spread through your tissues. If your circulation is poor, not all will be nourished.

One sign of poor circulation is constantly having cold hands. Your body focuses more on the major organs and gives less attention to your extremities. When this occurs, your sweat glands can become sluggish and blocked. Ginkgo can help promote good circulation and healthy sweating, as well as more acute sensitivity in your palm chakras.

Peppermint (*Mentha x piperita*) helps stimulate the eccrine glands and soothe an upset stomach. You may have noticed that when you have a cup of peppermint tea, your hands sometimes feel warmer. This doesn't happen all the time, but when it does, it shows that the energy in your palm chakras has been awakened. Your hands are now more sensitive to energy, and you can use them as a natural divination tool.

When you meet someone for the first time and shake hands, trust the impression that you receive. Peppermint tea will help you have more confidence in these intuitive messages.

Yarrow (*Achillea millefolium*) has an affinity for your circulatory system, but in a different way than the more warming herbs. Yarrow balances your circulation and has been used to regulate blood pressure. (Please always seek medical supervision for blood-pressure management.) As the yarrow helps your body relax, your blood vessels dilate. This healing property is also carried through to your eccrine glands. Yarrow induces your body to sweat by easing any tension within your circulatory system.

Y.E.P. is a popular, and very effective, herbal-tea combination that's been used to promote sweating for decades. *Y.E.P.* stands for **Y**arrow, **E**lder, and **P**eppermint. The three herbs work synergistically to clear the perspiratory pathways. This blend nourishes the eccrine glands and balances their function.

This tea is often used during fevers, too. It may sound counter-intuitive to take a hot tea when your body has already raised its temperature. However, this combination promotes sweating, which breaks the fever and helps your body cool.

Heart-Healthy Herbs

Herbal medicines have both physical and energetic properties. These heart-healthy herbs nourish and protect your physical heart, stimulate your heart chakra, and also heal you emotionally.

When you take herbs for cardiovascular health, it is important that you seek proper supervision. Trying to balance your blood pressure alone can be dangerous. Speak to your licensed naturopath or physician beforehand.

Astragalus (*Astragalus membranaceus*) is a tonic herb that nourishes the heart. It may balance blood pressure, as well as help you better cope with stress.

Astragalus is a wonderful regulator for the body. It corrects imbalances and helps you overcome any obstacles.

Take 25 drops of tincture twice per day as a restorative remedy.

Coleus (*Coleus forskohlii*) can help balance blood pressure and protect the heart. It supports healthy weight loss, especially in cases that fall under the umbrella of *metabolic syndrome.* People with this syndrome have excess weight, mostly on their midsection, as well as blood-pressure and blood-sugar issues—all of which can put extra strain on the heart. Coleus helps you shed the weight and get your metabolism back on track, while ensuring that your heart remains healthy.

Take 20 drops of tincture twice a day.

Dan Shen (*Salvia miltiorrhiza*) has a strong connection to the heart. It balances blood pressure and prevents your blood from becoming too thick. Dan Shen protects the heart and can reduce palpitations.

This herb can be helpful when people have a fiery energy about them, seeming angry and aggressive. A red face that comes from anger or high blood pressure can be a sign that this herb is needed.

Take 20 drops of tincture two or three times per day to quench the internal fire.

Hawthorn (*Crataegus monogyna*) is one of my (Robert's) favorite heart-healing herbs. I use it for both the physical and emotional heart.

On a physical level, it protects the heart muscle. It nourishes this precious organ, helping strengthen and regulate it. Emotionally and energetically, it soothes a broken heart. I've used it for healing grief; difficult relationships; and feelings of being taken advantage of by friends, family, or partners. Hawthorn has a gentle energy, like a comforting friend giving you support.

Take 15 drops of extract to mend your emotions.

Korean ginseng (*Panax ginseng*) is a tonic herb that deserves a great deal of respect. It stimulates and awakens the whole body. In contrast to the way caffeine stimulates, Korean ginseng heals and restores.

In recent times there has been a larger demand for ginseng products, as people feel they help with athletic performance. Ginseng may be useful for this purpose; however, the capabilities of this herb go far beyond making you run faster.

It nourishes the heart and clears feelings of debility. Korean ginseng allows you to cope with stressful situations in a healthy way, and has even shown an ability to increase mental alertness and memory. Taking a dose just before an exam can help you remember more information—an effect made even more powerful when you combine it with ginkgo.

Take 12 drops of tincture twice a day to reawaken your body and heart.

To heal and strengthen the endocrine glands, and therefore awaken the chakras, bring more peace into your life. Herbal medicines can help nourish these glands, but if the stress continues, it will only be a temporary fix. Practice regular meditation, spend time outside, and find ways to enjoy the beauty of each new day.

In Part III, we will cover a few methods to clear your energy and make your lifestyle conducive to intuitive insights.

Healing Your Body and Energy

CHAPTER NINE

DETOXING TO
CLEAR YOUR INTUITION

We are passionate about detoxing. We've seen it change our own lives for the better, but we've also taught thousands of people all over the world how to "clean up" their diets. When you release toxic emotions and unhealthy relationships . . . and truly detox from everything negative in your life . . . something incredible takes place.

Suddenly, your internal lie detector switches back on again. The voice of your Higher Self is the primary one you hear and connect to. Previously, that voice (which has been there all along) was clouded, and toxins were blocking your Divine communication. By detoxing, you're able to awaken and rediscover that wonderful energy and connection that's always been a very strong part of who you are.

Detoxing means different things to different people. Most think of it as eliminating virtually all foods, going on some kind of fast or juice diet, and then slowly reintroducing regular eating habits again.

For us, detoxing is a dietary and lifestyle overhaul. It means looking at every aspect of our lives, not just what we eat. We feel that the toxins from stress, anxiety, unforgiveness, and unresolved grief are just as damaging to your body as chemicals, alcohol, sugar, processed foods, and artificial sweeteners. We also acknowledge our sensitive nature and understand that harsh detox methods won't work for us.

Detoxing is a very, very powerful and life-changing step you may be guided to take. Chances are, if you're reading this book, then God and your angels have already been nudging you to make healthy changes that will increase and enhance your intuition.

Detoxing is not as hard as you might think it is. In our own personal experiences, we have detoxed from substances such as coffee and caffeine with absolutely no side effects. The angels were working with us step-by-step to make that transition peacefully and comfortably.

God and the angels know that if you are feeling uncomfortable, headachy, and moody as you let go of unhealthy foods, there's more risk that you'll jump right back in and start consuming them again. If, instead, you clear those things out of your diet and out of your life with very few or no side effects, then you'll do well. You'll follow through with that lifestyle change, and you'll feel the wonderful benefits as a result.

As you detox, please think about working with God and your angels. Don't feel like you have to go it alone. Detoxing is a combined effort, and when your loving support team is with you and urges you to succeed, you're far more likely to achieve all your goals.

When you begin the detox path, trust your own guidance as to what needs to be released first. The angels say that it's not about removing things and taking the fun stuff away. Instead, you are being *given* what you've been praying for: high energy and a sharp, keen sense of intuition. These are the things you truly want.

What the angels can see is that some foods and substances, and maybe even behaviors, are standing between you and your goals. When you've got toxic foods in your diet, a cloudiness follows you around. You miss or ignore all those beautiful miracles happening in front of you. If you remove whatever is blocking you—which might be sugar, wheat, or dairy—nothing is going to slow you down now. Everything your heart desires will be within reach.

The benefit of detoxing is not only clarity but higher energy—and it's *real* energy. You don't feel like you have to run off caffeine or other substances to get through the day. You don't feel like your energy peaks at a certain point and then plummets soon after. Instead, you feel energized all day long.

Don't listen to the ego voice that tells you detoxing is too hard. Don't pay attention when it says you'll experience uncomfortable headaches or excruciating withdrawal symptoms. The truth of the matter is that you will feel incredible joy and a strong sense of connection with the beings of love that surround you.

To begin your detox process, sit down and request a sign from the angels. Ask them very clearly what it is you need to focus on now by saying:

"Dear God and angels, please show me what changes you would like to see me make. Please give me signs that I will easily notice and understand in the physical world. I ask you to support me by making this transition comfortable for me. Please guide me to healthy choices and high-vibrational meals, while also removing temptation. I am willing to let go of all that no longer serves my highest good. Thank you."

Heaven may guide you to release particular foods or even environmental toxins from your life in order to awaken your intuitive gifts. This chapter covers steps to remove these substances and substitute healthy, intuition-enhancing alternatives.

Detoxing from Unhealthy Foods

There are certain types of food that appear to have more of a negative impact on our intuition than others. Four of these are *gluten, sugar, dairy products,* and *unhealthy fats.*

— **Gluten** is found in several different grains, including wheat, rye, and barley. There are also traces of gluten in oats; however, this may not rule out oats for you entirely. Some gluten-sensitive people can tolerate the amount in oats, so they're not something to immediately eliminate like the wheat, barley, and rye. Now, even if you aren't gluten intolerant, your body may still be sensitive to gluten. If you eat lots of breads, biscuits, cakes, and pasta, the gluten turns into glue on an energetic level. That glue sticks to the inside of your third eye, the center of clairvoyance and psychic sight, and makes it more difficult to see your angels and to connect on a spiritual level. As a gluten-free alternative to fulfill your need for grains, eat organic, non–genetically modified (non-GMO) rice (preferably whole brown or wild rice), corn, or quinoa.

— High amounts of **sugar** create crystals within your aura. Now, unlike healing crystals that send energy toward you, these sugar crystals pull energy out of your body. You may get headaches and feel generally fatigued or weakened. These sugar crystals drain you of your motivation. As God and your angels give you important messages that require action, there's no energy left to make the necessary changes.

— **Dairy products,** particularly concentrated forms such as cheese, can create a filminess over the third-eye area and a mucus-like coating over your entire aura. Dairy products will prevent you from being able to meditate on a deeper level. Your manifestation efforts are slowed, as you may find it hard to focus on your goals and aspirations.

We have not found any big difference between dairy products, whether coming from a cow, a goat, or another animal. We much prefer dairy alternatives, such as nut mylks or any of the other natural plant-based beverages.

— **Unhealthy fats** float through your aura and stick to all of your chakras, rather like cholesterol in the arteries. Consuming high amounts of unhealthy fats, like deep-fried foods or really oily snacks, will clog up and block your energy centers. This results in gut feelings that could be incorrect at times. Although in truth your intuition is always accurate, high amounts of unhealthy fats make it more challenging to decipher your true intuition and distinguish it from the ego voice.

We've helped many individuals who were abusing drugs and alcohol in order to hide from their gifts, but often people don't acknowledge that food is another form of addiction. They're caught in an addictive cycle where they can't seem to satisfy themselves, meal after meal. These people will go through different drive-through "restaurants" (and we use the term loosely) to try filling a void.

Although they may not realize it, the fast food and the chemicals involved in producing it are interfering with their spiritual gifts. It blocks out the nudges and messages from God and the angels. This dulling of their gifts is often one of the reasons why they were led to the fast food in the first place!

Why are sensitive people sometimes drawn to eating fast food? On a subconscious level, you might obscure your intuition and your internal lie detector for sensitive emotional reasons. Let's say, for example, that you're in an unhappy relationship. Your intuition is telling you that your partner may be unfaithful. Rather than acknowledging this fact or confronting your partner about these issues, you're drawn to fast foods to "stuff down" your feelings and muffle your inner voice. That way, it's "out of sight, out of mind."

Please don't abuse yourself in this way. You are far more valuable than you realize. You're perfect in truth, and created in God's image and likeness. In time you'll come to know that having your intuition switched on is one of the best assets you could ever ask for. Even though some messages can confront you with uncomfortable truths, they're always for your highest good. The loving guidance from your angels will help you understand your next steps in a comforting and reassuring way.

Common Cravings and How to Heal Them

Different food cravings can also give you clues as to what your body may be lacking nutritionally. Your body knows what it needs more of, so when you crave something specific to satiate yourself, it is intended to remedy that deficiency. However, with the processing of modern foods, it can be difficult to pinpoint what your body is truly after. The classic craving for chocolate and sugar is quite often due to a deficiency in magnesium. The raw cacao—the original form of chocolate before the sugar and fat are added to it—contains high amounts of magnesium. So on subconscious and intuitive levels, you're actually yearning for that very healthy superfood rather than the human-created, adulterated, sugar-filled version.

If you have cravings for a fatty, greasy kind of meal such as deep-fried foods, your body is in fact telling you that you're deficient in fat-soluble vitamins. Consume higher amounts of foods that contain these healing vitamins, such as avocado, this week. Try one teaspoon of beautiful organic, cold-pressed coconut oil per day for healthy fat intake. And include flaxseeds and chia seeds in your diet to give you a healthy supply of omega-3. (Take a look back at our recipe for Tasty Chia Pudding in Chapter 6.)

If you're craving higher amounts of carbohydrates, such as breads, this can be a sign that you're deficient in B vitamins. B vitamins come from complex whole grains, which is really what your body is asking for.

Listen to the signs that your body is giving you, as every single one of them is a clue. They will help you to discover the best, most nutritious way of eating that's absolutely perfect for you.

Here is a table of common cravings—including affirmations from my (Doreen's) book *Constant Craving*—along with the possible nutritional deficiencies behind them, and ways to better understand them.

Craving	Possible Deficiency	Foods to Enjoy	Energetic Meaning	Affirmation
Bread	B vitamins	Hearty soup with beans, lentils, and organic, non-GMO tofu A small handful of fresh sprouts such as chickpea, mung bean, or lentil	Feeling insecure. Desiring comfort and reassurance.	I am safe and secure. Love is in and around me.
Candy	Magnesium, B vitamins	Fresh juice Green smoothie A piece of fruit	Worries and insecurities. A desire for stronger romance. Fears around work.	I am safe and secure in all ways. I love myself, and others love me, too.
Carbohydrates	B vitamins, magnesium	Roasted root vegetables like beet, carrot, and sweet potato with the skin A small handful of raw nuts	Feeling unsupported. Unhappiness with the current direction of your life.	I am Divinely supported and guided in all ways.
Cheese	Vitamin E, vitamin A, vitamin D, calcium	Hummus with vegetable sticks Nut butter	Feeling exhausted and drained. A desire for comfort. Thoughts centered around the worst-case scenario.	I replace thoughts of fear with feelings of love. My true source of energy is infinite.

Craving	Possible Deficiency	Foods to Enjoy	Energetic Meaning	Affirmation
Chips/crisps	B vitamins, magnesium, essential fatty acids	Tamari almonds Pistachios	You feel stressed or anxious. You desire validation.	I trust that everything is going perfectly according to plan. I release feelings of being responsible for everyone and everything around me.
Chocolate	Magnesium	Cacao smoothie Carob Hazelnut mylk	Angry that love life is unsatisfactory. A longing for a storybook romance.	Perfect love resides within me now. I allow my inner sense of love to shine through.
Coffee	CoQ10, vitamin C	Dandelion-root coffee Chai (with natural ingredients and no sugar)	Your energy is drained by taking part in tasks that are meaningless to you. Burnout, disappointment, or resentment with your job.	I focus my thoughts on my true sense of energy that is within, and a part of me, now.
Dairy	Calcium, vitamin D, vitamin E, vitamin A	Various nut and seed mylks	Wanting to hide from current situations. You don't want to hear advice or opinions.	I allow myself to listen to helpful, supportive guidance. I am strong and ready to take the next step.
Deep-fried foods	Essential fatty acids, vitamin D, vitamin E, vitamin A	Avocado Macadamia mylk or a small handful of macadamias	A desire for a simpler life. Wanting to go back to basics.	I take my time and trust that solutions will present themselves to me.

Craving	Possible Deficiency	Foods to Enjoy	Energetic Meaning	Affirmation
Fries	Essential fatty acids, magnesium, vitamin D, vitamin E, vitamin A	Sweet potato and other roasted root vegetables like beets and carrots (with the skin on)	Feeling sad that your life doesn't match your dreams. Not even wanting to attempt to complete your goals.	I am filled with the warm flow of love through my heart. I use this force to propel me toward my dreams, starting now.
Pasta	B vitamins	Grated zucchini to make pasta-like strips, used raw or lightly warmed	Wanting comfort and reassurance.	I fill my entire being with loving thoughts.
Salt	Magnesium	Tamari almonds	A desire for more excitement and adventure. Too much predictability.	I allow new, exciting opportunities to come my way.
Soda	Calcium, B vitamins, vitamin C	Sparkling mineral water Herbal tea	Trying to stay motivated and energized.	When I follow my inner guidance, all of my needs are met.
Sugar	Magnesium, B vitamins	Smoothie with nut-mylk base Tasty Chia Pudding.	Focusing on negative thoughts and situations. Most tasks seem challenging.	I see the best outcome for everything I'm involved with.

Detoxing from Endocrine Disruptors

Certain chemicals can be harmful to your endocrine system, and therefore dramatically impact your intuition. We've written extensively about how to live a healthy, chemical-free life in our book *Angel Detox*. Some of these dangerous chemicals are used in common, everyday items. Below you'll read about how to avoid them, and later discover the natural alternatives you can make at home.

Triclosan

Triclosan is a highly toxic ingredient in antibacterial products. This synthetic antibacterial agent—found in toothpaste, cosmetics, and many liquid soaps—has been linked to immune- and endocrine-system issues. Studies have shown that triclosan can abnormally increase cell growth and cause elevated activity in the brain. It disrupts hormones in the body and also affects your muscles.

Researchers from the University of California, Davis, and the University of Colorado presented a paper at the Proceedings of the National Academy of Sciences that showed that triclosan impairs muscles—including the heart. They suggested that triclosan poses a very real risk to humans (Cherednichenko et al. 2012).

According to a large number of researchers, triclosan offers little benefit in antimicrobial and antibacterial hand washes. The process of rinsing your hands and rubbing them together dislodges bacteria and viruses, and the presence of triclosan doesn't make a significant difference in disinfecting. So if you have good hand-washing practices, you're already removing enough bacteria.

A study was completed on triclosan as an antibacterial hand wash, and the lead researcher admitted that it's only effective in uncommon situations where there are extremely high levels of bacteria. It's worth noting that the research was commissioned and funded by the American Cleaning Institute, a trade association for producers of cleaning products. Naturally, they have the most to gain from keeping this harmful chemical in their products.

Phthalates

Phthalates are common in plastics such as packaging, cling wrap, and bags. They can also be found in personal items like soap, shampoo, hair spray, and nail polish. These chemicals are added to plastics to make them stronger and more flexible. Phthalates have been linked to reproductive and endocrine-system issues.

Dioxins

Dioxins are highly toxic compounds produced after smelting, bleaching of paper pulp, and the manufacture of pesticides and herbicides. They pollute the environment and then end up in our food supply. Dioxins have a long life span in the body, taking over a decade to be released, so they collect in organisms and become more concentrated as they pass up the food chain.

Higher amounts of dioxins are present in dairy products, meat, fish, and shellfish. Regular testing of these foods ensures that the levels are "safe." In late 2008, authorities recalled tons of pork in Ireland when it was found to have more than 200 times the safe level of dioxins. Further research revealed that the feed given to the animals was contaminated.

To reduce your exposure to dioxins, enjoy a diet rich in plant foods and filter your water. We recommend gentle detoxing several times per year, as you could still absorb these chemicals from the environment. To learn how to detox effectively with the guidance of God and your angels, see our book *Angel Detox*.

BPA

Bisphenol A, or BPA, is another chemical used to make plastics stronger. The dangers of BPA-containing plastics have been well researched: This toxin leaches into foods and can lead to liver disturbances, heart disease, and reproductive issues. BPA is linked to several health concerns, including hormonal imbalances, liver abnormalities, and poor development of the brain in infants, as well as diabetes, breast cancer, heart disease, and infertility.

Many water bottles and food containers are made with BPA. As we mentioned in Chapter 5, BPA can also be present in canned foods, and the lining of cans can be made from BPA plastic. Harvard professors found that after eating canned soup once a day for five days, you increase your levels of BPA by 1,000 percent because the cans are lined with the chemical.

BPA bottles leach the chemical into the water they carry. When they're heated, like being left in a hot car or the grocery store's warm warehouse, they leach even more of this hazardous material. These plastics will be labeled with a recycling number 3 or 7, but these numbers alone don't mean that the bottle is harmful. A 3 means that the plastic is made with PVC, and a 7 implies that it doesn't fit into any other category. BPA-containing plastics are categorized both ways, but so are other plastics that may be safer. Still, it's best to avoid plastic bottles that have a number 3 or 7 on them. We recommend buying drinking water from glass bottles and storing your personal water in reusable glass bottles.

Many reputable water companies provide at-home water dispensers. Do your research, as the bottled water you drink may not be very good. The water supplied by your office is probably just as poor. Check the mineral analysis, and make sure it doesn't just have sodium and chloride. Some sodium is needed, but it shouldn't be the only mineral content. Good-quality water will also include small traces of calcium, magnesium, and potassium. With these minerals present, you'll be able to enjoy your water knowing your body can use it in metabolic functions.

Purified water and distilled water *sound* good, but these terms mean that all the microminerals have been removed. This leaves you with just H_2O. This is not ideal over the long term, but is significantly better than regular tap water. You can compromise in the meantime: filter your water, but add the minerals back in. Purchase good-quality Celtic, Atlantic, Himalayan, or Dead Sea salts. Add just a few grains to your drink bottle and shake well. These natural salts contain many minerals and electrolytes.

Here's a simple observation to make regarding your water quality. Notice how often you need to go to the bathroom after drinking. After a tall glass, you might need to visit the restroom 30 minutes later. With better-quality water, you may not need to relieve yourself for an hour or more. And when you do go, you'll release less than what you drank—the reason being that your body has utilized the water you ingested, and it hasn't simply passed through. Instead, it has been used in vital metabolic processes. You're receiving hydration and are putting the water you drink to good use.

Make drinking water fun by adding small amounts of freshly squeezed organic juice, or slices of fresh organic lemon and lime. Combine this with organic mint leaves for a refreshing treat on a warm day.

Natural Household-Cleaner and Personal-Care Alternatives

There are many wonderful natural products that you can use for cleaning and self-care. Most of the following are common household items or can be made very easily with simple ingredients. Learn how these products can be used in different ways to help you avoid chemical-laden products.

Lavender Oil

Essential oils are powerful disinfectants provided to us by nature. The oils offer physical cleaning properties along with metaphysical healing energies. This makes them the perfect choice for spiritually aware people like you.

An excellent antiseptic oil is lavender. Add lavender oil to a spray bottle full of water, shake well, and let sit for several hours. When you're ready to use it, shake vigorously before spraying the surfaces you wish to clean. After you finish, mist some more lavender over the surface for extra protection. The aroma is very soothing and helps calm anxieties and fears. It works to open your third-eye chakra and awakens your clairvoyance.

Tea Tree Oil

Tea tree oil is an exceptional antibacterial, antifungal, and antiseptic essential oil. It's perfect for cleaning and disinfecting, as it breaks through bacterial defenses. When bacteria group together, they secrete a substance that shields them from antiseptics. Tea tree oil works time and again for killing bacteria, as they seem unable to form a resistance to the natural oil.

Tea tree oil can be used in a whole host of ways. Pop a few drops in an aromatherapy diffuser to combat colds and flu. Spray it as an all-purpose cleaner by adding two teaspoons to two cups of water. Put this in a spray bottle and shake very well. Use it on kitchen countertops, in the shower, and to combat mold. If you don't care for the smell, add some geranium oil to the mixture.

Nontoxic Insect Repellents

Don't spray toxic insecticides in or around your home. They contain harmful chemicals that can disrupt your endocrine system and block your intuition. Instead, create your own natural, safe blend of insect repellent. Add ten drops of citronella essential oil, five drops of lavender oil, and five drops of geranium oil to a 3 fl. oz. (100 mL) spray bottle. Fill with water and shake well. Spray throughout your outdoor areas to naturally repel bugs.

You can spray this mixture on your skin, or make a lovely oil to use topically. In a base of organic cold-pressed extra-virgin olive oil or organic coconut oil, add the same essential-oil combination. Apply a small amount to your palms and then gently massage into your skin. You'll smell great, nourish your skin, and keep insects away.

You can use peppermint tea as a natural insect repellent as well. Add three teaspoons of dried, organic peppermint leaves for every cup of boiling water to a closed vessel like a teapot. Let it steep for half an hour and cool. When it's room temperature, you can pour it into a spray bottle. Use this outside on your plants and flowers to prevent bugs from munching on your blooms and salad greens—although once it's washed away through rain or watering, you'll need to re-mist with the refreshing scent of peppermint.

Baking Soda

Baking soda, or sodium bicarbonate, is a wonderful household item that's safe for you and your family to use. Baking soda balances the pH of anything it interacts with. Mix a teaspoon of baking soda in a glass of water. Rinse it in your mouth, swish it around, and then spit into the sink. Your breath will be fresh, as the baking soda neutralizes odors and balances your oral health.

You can create an exfoliant that's gentle enough for daily use. Make a paste by adding a little water to some baking soda. Then, gently rub in circular motions over the neck and face. You can give yourself a whole-body scrub, too! This is also a great hand cleanser for stubborn dirt or odors.

As a natural deodorant, baking soda can be lightly applied to your underarms. Just use the dry powder and pat away any excess. It can neutralize other odors, too. Keep an open box in the refrigerator. After a month or two, dispose of the box by pouring it down the drain. As you do so, let the warm water run from the faucet. It will remove any drain smells and make your sink fresh. Also, you can sprinkle some baking soda in the bottom of trash cans to avoid unwelcome smells.

These are some cleaning uses:

- Sprinkle some baking soda onto a damp sponge and scrub the shower and bathroom as normal. Then, rinse off and wipe dry. The tiles will sparkle like new, and there isn't any need to wear a face mask since there are no harsh chemicals!

- For baked-on food, sprinkle a few spoonfuls of baking soda into the pan. Add a little water and let it soak. You'll find that food washes off much easier.

- Clean your oven by making a paste with baking soda. Apply it to stubborn areas and then let it sit overnight. In the morning, use a wet sponge to clean the inside. Remove any debris and wipe with a damp sponge.

- Mop your floors with a solution of a half cup baking soda in a bucket of warm water. Or dust baking soda over the carpet and leave overnight. The next day, vacuum up the powder for a fresh-smelling room.

Hand Spray

During the day you can come into contact with a multitude of germs. Shopping carts, door handles, restroom surfaces, and handrails are all areas that can have high concentrations of germs. By cleaning your hands often, you can ensure that you and your family maintain first-rate levels of hygiene.

Regular hand sanitizers are filled with harsh chemicals and toxins, including triclosan. These products should be avoided! There are, however, natural hand sanitizers that are made from botanical cleansers. If you choose to use one of these, please read the labels carefully, as many still contain synthetic fragrances and chemicals.

After doing some research, we've decided that it's safest, and often easiest, for us to make our own hand cleanser. Add 200 drops (about two teaspoons) of tea tree essential oil to a 3 fl. oz. (100 mL) bottle filled with water. Shake it vigorously to help the oils give their cleansing properties to the water. You can make your spray more effective by adding an emulsifying agent. Many quality essential-oil suppliers will have something you can mix with the oils to make them combine better with water. Make sure they're always from natural, nonallergenic sources.

Carry this spray (or decant into more convenient-size bottles), and spray your hands (or applicable surfaces) as you need to. The natural antiseptic property of tea tree oil will remove any bacteria.

Raw (or Virgin) Coconut Oil

Virgin coconut oil is a wonderful natural skin-care item. Your skin readily absorbs this nourishing oil and uses it to repair connective tissue. It can help minimize fine lines and bring a youthful glow to your complexion. Apply the oil to your face and all over your body.

You can use organic virgin coconut oil in cooking, too. Unlike other oils, it won't go rancid or form unhealthy trans fats when heated. You can cook with coconut oil at high temperatures, and it still remains nutritious. Your body easily digests this oil, and it can help you lose weight. As you replace other oils with natural coconut oil, you'll find that you have energy to be more active, which will speed up your metabolism.

If you're being strongly guided to detox, you may find our book *Angel Detox* helpful. We cover releasing toxins from all areas of your life physically, emotionally, and spiritually by combining energetic-healing methods with naturopathic advice.

Going through a detox does for your physical body what changing the oil does for a car. Releasing chemicals from your diet and focusing on natural, plant-based foods clears away a fogginess and hesitation in believing your own Divine guidance. Even if your diet is clean, healthy, and organic, you'll benefit from regular detoxing. After all, you may be exposed to toxins as you complete your daily activities. There are exhaust fumes from cars, cigarette smoke in the streets, and chemical-laden air fresheners in malls. There could even be toxins in your workplace. Detoxing a few times throughout the year can be a wonderful experience. You will feel uplifted as you let go of toxins that are clouding your vision and blocking your happiness.

CHAPTER TEN

How to Clear Your Chakras

Your chakras absorb and send out energy simultaneously, and over time they may become clogged with lower vibrations. The places you visit, the people you interact with, and what you hear and read influence your chakra system.

Visualize an air conditioner as it draws in and sends out air at the same time. Its purpose is to cool the air before releasing it back into the room. It draws in *any* air around it—whether cold, hot, clean, or dusty. Like an air conditioner, you absorb the energy from the space you're in. Your chakras process the energy and then send out the resonant vibrations.

Your chakras are akin to the filter of the air conditioner. If it becomes dusty, the unit will no longer work properly. Similarly, if your chakras become congested with negative energy, it impedes the natural flow of energy around your body. That's why it's important to clear your chakras regularly to ensure that you always have a prime sense of vitality and keen, accurate intuition.

Like attracts like, and this is true for energy. If your chakras are shrouded in negativity, it seems as if you attract *more* negative situations. Tasks are more difficult to complete, procrastination is high, and a general lack of motivation afflicts you.

Conversely, if your chakras are filled with light, you attract more positive energy. You're met with greater joy, compassion, and love.

The words you speak are overlaid with an uplifting energy that helps to heal. People will comment on how you're glowing with happiness!

The angels have told us that there's nothing the darkness fears more than the light. Like flicking a switch, the light instantly dispels the darkness. When your chakras are glowing with light, the particles of negative energy have nowhere to hide. Your body is given a "nonstick coating," which makes it difficult for lower vibrations to take hold.

You have a Divine life purpose that only *you* can complete. Realizing that the negative energies and words from others can't slow you down, you are capable of achieving incredible things. By shining your light, you clear a path ahead of you to be paved with love.

There are a number of things you can do to ensure your chakras are always shining their brightest. We recommend clearing your chakras on a regular basis to make certain lower energies won't impact you or your intuitive gifts. How often you need to clear is dependent on the types of things you encounter each day. If you find yourself surrounded by negative, complaining, draining people, you will have to clear your chakras more frequently.

Strengthening Your Chakras' Immune System

If you're already sensitive to feelings, you may wonder why you'd want to increase your clairsentience. You may fear being overwhelmed with sensations, especially since you intensely feel energies.

It's true that clairsentient people, sometimes called *empaths,* are highly sensitive to everything. They avoid crowds because they can feel the energies and emotions of every person present. They like to spend time with loving, happy people. As they sit with somebody, if that individual is experiencing physical pain, the clairsentient person may also start to feel those symptoms.

There's no benefit in feeling somebody else's pain, so if you do, please call upon your angels and ask for shielding. That way, instead of physical pain, you'll receive a sign such as a tingling sensation, an air-pressure change, or an area of warmth. You are still able to receive the insight, but you no longer have pain attached to the message.

Clairsentience is a protective tool of those who are highly sensitive. With clairsentience, you get an instant sense of who's trustworthy and who should be avoided. Around each chakra, there's also a transparent protective energy field that functions like a shielding barrier. This becomes your first line of defense against negativity.

It's similar to your body's immune system. This spiritual immunity helps clear and transmute negative energies before they can have any effect on you. The light from your chakras shines through to dissolve all darkness.

In busy, stressful environments, clairsentients are like sponges that absorb that energy. The entire nervous, limbic, and endocrine systems are involved with stress management. Anytime you are afraid, they release stress hormones to create homeostasis. However, if the stress goes on too long, the body becomes unbalanced or even sick from an overproduction of cortisol, adrenaline, histamine, and other stress hormones.

But with healthy care for your chakras and corresponding endocrine glands, your clairsentience is even clearer. The chakras become self-cleaning, and—even though it's important to be discerning about whom you spend time with, and what you eat or drink—you are not as vulnerable to negativity.

When you care for your chakras as we have been discussing throughout this book, their "immune system" is strengthened. Negative energy is really low-vibrational energy, and the particles can't pass through the protective field of healthy chakras. Like a lock and key, only the high vibrations of love, compassion, joy, generosity, and the like can enter when the chakras are well maintained.

Chakra-Clearing Methods

Each chakra has its own vibration, so we've listed specific tools to clear them individually here. We also explain techniques for clearing and balancing all your chakras at once, as well as how you can gain the most benefit from each method.

Meditation

Meditation allows you to use your inner vision and psychic sight to assess your chakras. Start by visualizing each chakra as a spinning circle of light in your mind's eye. At first, you may or may not be able to see the color associated with each energy center. With practice, though, you'll soon pick up on the colors and the health of each chakra through meditation.

Notice how rapidly the chakra is spinning in a clockwise direction. Is it fast or slow? Do you intuitively feel as if it could be moving more quickly? If so, use your intention to make the energy spin faster.

You may be aware of areas of darkness either in or around the chakra. Using the power of your intention, see a bright white light (or picture the color associated with the chakra) and watch as it dissolves the darkness. You may be more of a *feeling* person, so sense within your body that the changes are taking place.

Here are a few meditations we've found highly effective at clearing our chakras.

Healing Blooms

During your meditation, visualize each chakra as a rosebud waiting to blossom. Imagine the flower opening up; as you do, so too will your chakra. For example, see in your mind's eye a yellow rosebud blossoming in your solar plexus. This vision clears and awakens that chakra.

Pools of Light

Imagine an ancient pool of water, surrounded by mystical carvings and symbols. The water transforms into a ruby red light (the color of your root chakra). Visualize yourself stepping into the pool of light and swimming around as you enjoy the energy.

After a few moments, you carefully step out and walk up a few stairs to find another pool of light. This time the energy is glowing orange (resonating with the sacral chakra). Enjoy swimming in the light, before you continue the process with the other

*pools of light—yellow . . . green . . . light blue . . . dark blue . . .
violet red . . . and purple.*

Archangel Michael Vacuuming

One of Archangel Michael's chief purposes is to clear away negative energy. He lifts and removes all fear and transforms it back
into love.

During one of my (Doreen's) meditations, I received a vision of
Archangel Michael suctioning away negativity. As I continued to work
with him, he cleared my energy by placing a tube in through my
crown chakra and suctioning away fear. The device he was using can
only be described as a spiritual vacuum!

Since then I've taught thousands of others how to use this clearing method, with fantastic results. Archangel Michael will work with
anyone who asks him for help.

*Start by allowing yourself to relax and find a comfortable
position. Next, call upon Archangel Michael by saying:*

*"Dear God and Archangel Michael, please vacuum
away all fear energy from my body and aura. I ask you
to pay particular attention to my chakras and ensure
they are filled with light. Thank you."*

*You may see or feel Archangel Michael pulling out darkness
and negativity as he clears you. Be willing to release it all, without judgment or hesitation. He will move up through each of
your chakras one by one.*

*Once you feel the clearing is complete, Michael will pour a
crystal white light into your body, infusing it with love and keeping you clear.*

Archangel Metatron's Sacred Beam of Light

Archangel Metatron helps bring balance to your life. One of the ways he does so is through clearing your chakras. If your energy centers are in perfect order, all areas of your life mirror that perfection.

Metatron uses a beam of light to cleanse negativity. The beam comes from the heavens and has the ability to change color. Clairvoyantly, you may also see sacred symbols flowing through it.

Find a quiet space where you can comfortably relax. Then call upon Archangel Metatron by saying:

"Dear God and Archangel Metatron, please cleanse and balance all of my chakras using your sacred beam of light. Thank you."

Now see or feel a bright white beam of light coming down from Heaven. The beam enters through the top of your head and instantly fills your body with light. This cleansing light illuminates all of the cells within your beautiful body.

Archangel Metatron then brings the beam of light out through your root chakra. As he does so, the beam transforms into a magnificent ruby red. The red light clears all lower energies from your root chakra.

Once this clearing is complete, he moves up to your sacral chakra, where the beam comes through as a vibrant orange.

He continues with all of your remaining chakras, and the beam adapts to the matching color each time:

- *Yellow for solar plexus*
- *Green for heart*
- *Light blue for throat*
- *Dark blue for third eye*
- *Violet red for ear*
- *Purple for crown*

When Archangel Metatron has finished clearing your chakras, the beam flows back up into the heavens, leaving you sparkling with light.

Spinning Rings

For this meditation, you take yourself on an astral flight through rings of color. Each color you fly through clears the corresponding energy center, leaving you balanced at the end. By drawing your attention to the specific color of each chakra, the rings allow your energy to respond to its vibration. Clairvoyantly, you see the vortex of your chakra open up and pull in that vibration, simultaneously pushing out any old fear or negativity that's taking up space.

Begin by focusing on your breathing as you gently close your eyes. Sit in this relaxed state for several minutes. Now allow your awareness to take you up above the ground and into the sky. Your weightless body can effortlessly glide through the air.

You see a red spinning ring up ahead, glowing with light. It is large enough for you to easily fly through. Take yourself through the ring as it clears your root chakra.

A little farther ahead, you see an orange spinning ring. Using the power of your intention, you are able to smoothly fly through . it as your sacral chakra is cleared.

Continue this flight through all of your chakras:

- *Yellow for solar plexus*
- *Green for heart*
- *Light blue for throat*
- *Dark blue for third eye*
- *Violet red for ear*
- *Purple for crown*

Breath of Color

Just like the spinning-rings meditation, the breath of color balances your chakras by focusing your awareness on their colors.

Quiet your mind and focus on your breathing. Take relaxed breaths in and out, not forcing anything. Allow yourself to calm before you begin.

Start with the color red and visualize breathing in ruby-red light. As you exhale, you release any blocks from your root chakra. Repeat this for three more breaths.

Then shift your focus to the color orange, breathing in the orange light . . . and exhaling all negative energy. Repeat that process for at least three breaths, then move your focus to the color yellow . . . green . . . light blue . . . dark blue . . . violet red . . . and, finally, purple.

Crystals

Crystals are another way to awaken your chakras. These healing stones carry a powerful vibration that resonates with your energy centers. You can place the crystal on, or above, the specific chakra you're working with. You can also hold the stone in your hand, as its energy will flow to wherever it will do its best healing.

Think of crystals as you would a person. Treat them with respect, and ask them politely to help you with your desires. Doing so helps create a spiritual bond between you. It's that connection that allows the healing energy to flow.

Always clear your crystal before use to rid it of old energies. There are many ways to do so, such as:

- Passing the stone through the smoke of your favorite incense.

- Laying it on the grass for at least four hours. (Do make sure the chosen crystal won't magnify the rays of the sun and start a fire.)

- Misting it with flower essences.

- Placing it in a bowl and covering it with fresh flower petals. The flowers clear the energy and recharge the stone.

You can also ask God and the angels to clear the energy of your crystal. Archangel Michael dissolves all past associations with the stone and revives its healing power. Hold the crystal in your receptive hand (the one you don't naturally write with) and allow your dominant hand to hover over it so your palms are facing each other. Next, ask for Michael's help by saying:

"Dear God and Archangel Michael, please send your violet ray of purifying light into this crystal. May it be cleansed of all old energies and reawakened as a sacred healing tool. Thank you."

Visualize the violet light cleansing the crystal until you feel that the process is complete. This revitalizes the crystal and activates its healing potential.

There are many ways to work with crystals, and we encourage you to trust your intuition. Here are some of our favorites that we've found effective:

Clear-Quartz Point Clearing

Find a clear quartz crystal that has a single termination (meaning that it has a point at one end). It needn't be big—a crystal two inches long will do.

We encourage you to try this technique with a smaller, less expensive quartz point before you decide to purchase a larger crystal. That way you know this method resonates with you first. The benefit of a larger stone is that it's able to channel more healing energies. A smaller piece is equally effective; it might just take a few more minutes to clear your chakras.

- Take your cleansed crystal with you to a place where you won't be disturbed. Close your eyes and take several relaxing, deep breaths.

- Hold the quartz crystal in your dominant hand (the hand you naturally write with) and point it at your root chakra. You'll feel the energy when the crystal is four to six inches away from your physical body.

- Imagine a bright red beam of light coming through the crystal and clearing your root chakra. See any areas of darkness being dissolved. You may also intuitively move the crystal in a clockwise direction to stimulate the circulation of energy.

- Continue clearing your root chakra with the crystal until you feel it is complete. Then, move up to the sacral chakra. See an orange beam of light coming through the quartz crystal as it magnifies your intentions.

- Repeat the same process for each of your chakras—up through the solar plexus, heart, throat, third eye, ears, and crown.

Once finished, it feels good to again take the crystal through your chakras, following your breath. As you breathe in, trace the crystal from the top of your head down to the root. Then as you exhale, bring the energy up with your breath, lifting the crystal from the root to the crown.

Laying on of the Stones

Laying on of the stones is an ancient practice where crystals are placed in specific areas of your body. Traditionally the recipient of this ritual is draped in a light white cloth, with crystals adorning his or her body. While this is a beautiful experience, it isn't necessary in order to get wonderful healing from your crystals.

- First, gather a collection of crystals you feel guided to work with. You can choose one for each of the chakras, and then some additional stones to lay around your body. Or just choose a couple that you feel drawn to right now.

- Resting in your bed or on the floor, carefully place the crystals one by one on your body. It doesn't matter if they aren't perfectly in position, as they tend to find their own resting place anyway.

- Lie back and close your eyes, and allow the energy of the crystals to cleanse and balance you. The vibrations from the crystals will awaken your chakras, bringing greater clarity and focus.

- After 15 minutes—or longer if you're enjoying yourself— slowly gather up the crystals from your body. Take several cleansing breaths before gradually sitting up.

Energy Balance

Sometimes your chakras aren't blocked; they're just out of balance. This exercise helps create balance throughout all levels of your energetic space:

- Intuitively choose a crystal you're drawn to. You'll want two of the same type, similar in size.

- Hold one in your left hand and the other in your right. Close your eyes and relax your breathing. Starting with the right hand, feel the energy go from the crystal, through your body, and over to the left hand.

- After a few moments, feel the energy move in the opposite direction. Your left hand builds the energy and sends it across to the right hand.

- Repeat this exercise for several minutes, gently sending energy from one side of your body to the other.

- Next, try sending the energy in a circular pattern. Feel it go from the crystal in your right hand in an upward arc over to the left hand. Then, from there, it creates a downward arc back to the right hand. Allow the energy to flow in this way for several minutes.

- Change the direction in which the energy flows. From the left hand, send the energy in an upward arc to the right hand, then in a downward arc to the left hand again. By allowing the energy to circulate in both directions, you balance your chakras.

Flowers

Flowers are a beautiful tool to clear your chakras and uplift your spirit. Each and every one has a connection to God and the angels. So when you work with flowers, you are bringing the Divine and the power of nature into your life. You can hold on to a flower while meditating to clear your energy.

Certain flowers resonate with your individual chakras, and just by holding a bloom over that area, you'll feel the old energy lifting. We've listed flowers for each chakra in the Appendix.

Photographs

Fresh flowers are heavenly to work with due to the subtle perfume they give off. Photos and pictures of flowers can be just as effective and powerful, though. The photo carries the same vibration as the fresh flower, as its essence has been captured.

Simply wave a picture of the flower (or one of the cards from our *Flower Therapy Oracle Cards* deck) through your aura, as though you are fanning away the negative energies. The flowers, and the angels of nature, will do all the work for you. You may intuitively feel guided to pause over certain areas of your body where the flower needs to do more clearing.

Aura Stroking

Choose a flower that you are drawn to work with. Powerful clearing flowers include the white rose, dianthus, lotus, bird-of-paradise, African violet, and iris.

Slowly take the flower through your aura and over each of your chakras. Allow yourself to be intuitively guided as you do so. If you feel the urge to pause over a particular area, trust that the flower may need to clear more energy from that region.

Aura stroking with the flower brings a freshness and vibrancy to your auric field. The blossom naturally pulls out all lower energies from your chakras. When the process is complete, you can place the flower in a vase or leave it outside in nature.

You may find that the flowers you use for aura stroking wilt faster. This is because they absorb the negative energy and dissolve it within themselves. This is a powerful gift that Mother Nature and God have given us. Enjoy working with flowers, as it is their Divine destiny to help you.

Single-Flower Meditation

When you sit with a single flower, it shares its story with you. It brings you peaceful new insights that help you understand your current situation.

Take a flower of your choosing to a comfortable space where you won't be disturbed. Hold the flower in your hands and observe its natural beauty. Admire the color, the shapes, and the delicate perfume it has to share.

Ask a question that's on your mind, or perhaps request guidance about how to keep your chakras clear and balanced.

It's a good idea to have a pen and paper on hand. This way you can write down anything that comes through via your thoughts, feelings, or visions.

Sweeping Away

Sometimes a simple gesture can be enough to shift lower vibrations. We use a method I (Doreen) was shown by the angels, called the *Source*-erer's or the *Source*-eress's sweep. (*Source*, of course, is God's loving power.) It's an action you do with your dominant hand (the one you naturally write with). The best way to describe it would be like you're shooing an insect away from food. You make that motion three times in front of the chakra you wish to clear.

It's a perfect way to clear the energy when people say, "You must be getting sick," and other negative or limiting things. You can also sweep negative particles from your aura.

We've had the pleasure of signing books for participants at our workshops. The lines are often long, although we don't mind, as it's a fun way for us to connect with people more personally. After a while, though, they often start to make well-intentioned, sympathetic comments such as "You must be getting tired," "I'm sure your hand hurts by now," and other negative affirmations. Of course, these sweet people don't mean any harm by what they say; however, we know the power that words can have. So as we hear these statements, we quickly clear the negativity by doing the sweep.

Music

Sound and music can affect your mood and emotions. By listening to positive music, you expand and elevate your energy.

The great scientific mind Albert Einstein was also influenced by music. He said that he would turn to it when he felt he had reached a roadblock in his work. The vibrational frequencies of the music would awaken his intuition and give him new insights. Einstein even once remarked, "It [the theory of relativity] occurred to me by intuition, and music is the driving force behind this intuition. My parents had me study the violin from the time I was six. My new discovery is the result of musical perception."

Likewise, Dr. Mitchell Gaynor, director of Medical Oncology and Integrative Medicine at the Cornell Cancer Prevention Center in

New York, believes in the power of music. He beautifully explains his thoughts in his book *The Healing Power of Sound:*

> If we accept that sound is vibration, and we know that vibration touches every part of our physical being, then we understand that sound is "heard" not only through our ears but through every cell in our body. . . . [S]ound works on the physical level because it so deeply touches and transforms us on the emotional and spiritual planes. . . . I believe that sound can play a role in virtually any medical disorder, since it redresses imbalances on every level of physiologic functioning.

When you listen to your favorite artists, and maybe even start to sing along, your chakras clear themselves. It's the high vibration of joy that transmutes all negative particles.

Each of your chakras resonates with a specific musical note. (Please see the "Healing Insights for Each Chakra" section in the Appendix.) You can listen to the magical music of crystal and Tibetan singing bowls, or tuning forks. Each is made to sound a particular note and heals the corresponding chakra.

Listening to this angelic music causes your chakra to vibrate. This vibration lifts out fear, negativity, and darkness, while simultaneously awakening and activating your energy center. As you listen to high-energy, positive music, your intuition becomes clear and accurate.

Affirmations

Similar to music, your words have a profound impact on your energy. If you speak with a positive, uplifting attitude, you'll find wonderful opportunities coming your way. If you constantly complain about the bad things around you or the negatives in your life, you'll appear to attract challenges.

Whatever you speak about is what you create more of. So choose to talk about the best possible scenarios, the easiest way to do something, or how you've grown and learned from an experience.

When you describe something in the present tense that perhaps hasn't happened yet, or that you're trying to attract, it's called an *affirmation.* Affirmations are sentences that you repeat to yourself either aloud or in your mind. That said, there's something powerful about speaking the words aloud. In the previous chapter, we presented some affirmations designed to banish cravings during your detox. The vibration of those words ripples outward and sets positive experiences in motion.

(We've included helpful affirmations specific to each chakra in the Appendix.)

Prayer

You never have to overcome anything on your own. You have the support of your heavenly helpers—God and the angels. When you call upon them, they will lovingly answer your prayers.

As we've mentioned, the Law of Free Will states that you must ask for assistance before God can intervene. Praying is the perfect way to grant permission for Divine help.

When you pray, do so with your heart. The words are not as important as your intention. If you rush a prayer, you do yourself a disservice. Take your time when you communicate with God.

The best way to pray is to surrender the result to Heaven. Don't worry about what will happen, or when. Instead, have faith and trust that everything will unfold in the most perfect way.

Close your eyes and take a few deep breaths. Relax, and then begin your prayer.

Prayer to Clear and Balance All Chakras

"Dear God, I ask You to please fill my body with Your light. I welcome Your Divine love. I call upon my guardian angels, as well as Archangels Michael and Raphael.

Please clear me of lower energies and awaken each of my chakras.

I ask that you please release all fear connected to money, security, and safety from my root chakra.

Please clear my sacral chakra by balancing my physical and mental desires, as well as my creativity.

God and angels, please release all forms of fear connected to my self-esteem, self-confidence, and personal power from my solar-plexus chakra.

I ask you to please lift away any blocks to expressing and receiving love from my heart chakra.

Please awaken my throat chakra by dissolving any negativity connected with speaking my truth, writing, and all areas of communication.

Please clear all lower energies surrounding my intuition, clairvoyance, and spiritual gifts from my third-eye chakra.

I ask you to dispel all darkness from my ear chakras by releasing other people's judgments and hurtful words.

God, please clear all fear from my crown chakra by reminding me that I am always Divinely supported, protected, and guided.

*Thank You so much for this clearing.
I love and appreciate You."*

CHAPTER ELEVEN

OPTIMIZING YOUR NUTRITION-FOR-INTUITION LIFESTYLE

As you make the transition from processed, human-made foods and venture into the world of natural produce, your body will instantly start to feel the effects. You might imagine that you'd go through an uncomfortable detoxification where you get headaches and withdrawal symptoms—but, in our experience, this isn't the case. For highly sensitive people like you, the angels support your transition to healthy food. (Of course, the angels are with people who aren't aware of their sensitive, spiritual nature, too. Unfortunately, though, the messages and guidance being sent to them by God and their angels aren't being heard.)

Call upon Heaven by saying:

> *"Dear God and angels, I ask you to be by my side right now. Please talk to me loudly and clearly as I go shopping for food, and as I prepare meals to eat. I ask that you show me the high-energy foods that are right for my family and me. Please allow me to easily absorb and digest these natural creations. I ask that any form of detox*

*that takes place, as my body becomes healthier and
healthier, be comfortable to me. I know that as I choose
nutritious options, my spiritual abilities will be enhanced,
my intuition will become stronger and clearer, and I'll be
guided every step of the way as to which foods
will be best for me. Thank you."*

God and the angels accentuate feelings that encourage you—that help you take the next step in your journey—and assure you that you are safe and protected. You'll gain a sense of knowing that your inner voice is not coming from a place of fear and has a higher purpose. Communicating with Heaven endows you with the courage to follow the guidance of that voice. Receiving the message is only one part of that equation. Taking action is the next step.

As you embark upon a detox or new nutrition-for-intuition lifestyle choices, you can optimize how you work with your angels by being conscious of the energies associated with each day of the week.

The Spiritual Properties of the Days of the Week

Have you ever tried to complete a particular task or perhaps start your healthy new eating plan, yet immediately found it really challenging? Maybe you sat down to pen that beautiful, heartfelt letter to someone you care about, but just couldn't find the right words.

Why is that?

Well, you see, every day of the week has its own energetic feeling about it. On one particular day, the energy of love is stronger. On a different day, the energy of your spiritual gifts and your motivation is stronger.

Now, this doesn't mean you can't talk about love or spirituality unless it's a certain day of the week. By becoming aware of these daily energy influences, though, you set yourself up for success from the very beginning and ensure that your efforts have the best effect and the most powerful outcome.

We want to share with you our intuitive feelings about each day of the week, the energies they contain, and which angels guide them.

Monday

Monday is a day of learning from experience. The first day of the workweek is the start of our routine. As such, so many people with a goal of implementing their healthy eating plan, being more nutritionally conscious, or commencing an exercise regime will usually kick things off on a Monday. However, the very beginning of the week is a time when you process your emotions, and the energy of Monday can be quite heavy and tough.

We often have big experiences toward the end of the week and over the weekend that we haven't fully integrated. As Monday comes around and, along with it, the start of a new week at work, we're left with the tail end of that intense energy. So, on Monday, we process everything that's happened. We catch our breath again, and we learn from the experiences that have taken place.

This means, then, that if you try to start something new on a Monday, it's going to be challenging. It's not impossible, but it won't be as easy as it could be, because you're still dealing with the remnants of last week.

Fortunately, one of the angels connected to Monday is **Archangel Azrael**, who helps us heal through any old energies and emotions, as well as grief. Now, our grief may stem from the loss of a loved one, or perhaps from energy of disappointment around how a friend treated us over the weekend.

Archangel Uriel, a wonderful angel of inspiration and learning, also guides Monday. He helps us form new ideas and have lightbulb moments. This insight allows us to understand what has transpired over that previous week so that we don't have to continue the same lesson over and over again.

You may have found yourself going through repetitive situations in the past. All of this is aimed at helping with your soul's growth. The angels want you to succeed and master each lesson involved, so if you miss any, you have to repeat that experience again. Once you gain understanding, you no longer have to go through the same cycle. Uriel gives you motivation and the inspiration to know that this could be your best week so far.

Tuesday

Tuesday is a day of preparation, an interval in which we start to gather the things we need to achieve our goals and dreams. It's a time when we get in touch with important contacts and send those e-mails requesting further information for planning purposes.

Tuesday is also a day of rejuvenation, because our bodies are now at peace. We've cleared through the old energy of the previous week, and we no longer have to deal with those issues. This is the perfect moment for us to focus on allowing healing to take place. Of course, our chief healing angel is **Archangel Raphael.** By working with Raphael on a Tuesday, we're able to absorb every ounce of healing— emotional, spiritual, and physical—that we need. Naturally, Raphael is available to us every day of the week, and healing is possible at every moment, but on Tuesdays our bodies are that much more receptive.

If you've been struggling with a particular health issue or if you feel like your prayers aren't being heard, take some extra time on this day to see a like-minded, supportive practitioner or a comforting friend who can help you understand which steps to take next.

Archangel Sandalphon also guides this day. Sandalphon is the angel who ensures that all your prayers are carried up to Heaven. Every single one that you send out is being heard and responded to. It's just that here on Earth, it can sometimes be easy to miss the subtlety of the response. This doesn't mean that the prayers have gone unanswered. Rather, it means that you may be limiting the way in which you can receive that Divine guidance. So when you pray for healing—or for anything at all—always remain open with regard to the result. Don't limit what the angels and God can create for you.

Wednesday

Wednesday is an excellent day to launch new ideas. It's a time to take guided action by putting all our creative thoughts into motion. We take that leap of faith onto the next leg on our journey so that we're no longer rooted in the same place we were this time last week. Wednesday is a motivational day that propels us forward toward our goals. That's why it's the ideal day to begin a new healthy eating routine, or to start on any goals that require commitment to some kind of daily practice.

What the angels have told us is that midweek is that perfect time when we've settled into the week's energy. We know what the feeling of it is going to be like, and we have prepared ourselves emotionally, spiritually, and physically to take on the challenges that may be ahead of us. On Monday, in contrast, we're still finding our feet, and it can feel like we're on rocky ground. If we try to change something then, it may be harder for us to see it through, because there are too many opportunities for stress to overwhelm us. The angels shine a light upon Wednesday and say that this is the day to move ahead, to leave the past behind, and to start fresh.

The angels that oversee Wednesday are **Archangels Metatron** and **Chamuel,** who guide us to stick with what we're trying to achieve and find what we're looking for.

Metatron helps create balance in every area of your life. He will help you:

- Find the time you need to create whatever it is you're trying to create

- Harmonize your energy so that you're able to follow your guidance

- Trust your intuition with respect to what you're feeling called to do

Archangel Chamuel is our "finding" angel. He will help you track down whatever it is you need in order to succeed:

- The perfect people to bring on board

- The money to support your idea

- The confidence to follow through with that goal

Whatever it is, Chamuel can locate it, because nothing is hidden from the eyes of God. (Remember that our angels are that energy extension of our Creator.) Archangel Chamuel can see very clearly what you need.

Thursday

Thursday is a time when you really start to buckle down and get the job done. It is a day for meaningful work—not just the everyday tasks that you're required to do, but the stuff that your heart is calling for. Dedicate today to whatever you dream of doing in your spare time. This is a time to fulfill your life purpose. Whatever it is that you have contracted to do in this lifetime is meant to happen now. There's no point in waiting—until retirement, until there's X amount of dollars in the bank account, until the time feels just right—because the world needs what you have to offer . . . *today.* That's why Thursday is such a motivating, powerful day of the week—it reminds you of why you are here. It reminds you that you have a very important path ahead of you, and you need to be spending time on that in order to fulfill all that you've signed up for.

Thursday is a day guided by **Archangel Raziel,** our spiritual-teaching angel. Raziel can call up past-life experiences and help us unlock the mysteries of our souls. Archangel Raziel was with you when you signed the contract for this lifetime, so he knows precisely why you are here and what you're being guided to do. Thursday is a wonderful time to meditate with Archangel Raziel and ask for guidance if you feel unsure about your spiritual path.

Archangel Gabriel also guides us on Thursday. Gabriel is our angel of communication, helping us with writing, speaking, and teaching. Thursday is a powerful time to share the important truths within your soul that you sense other people need to know. Gabriel will help you structure sentences and express yourself in words that everyone you communicate with will understand. Your messages will be received loud and clear.

Friday

Friday is the end of the workweek for most people, and the energy around it is one of completion. By allowing ourselves to bring to a close what was taking most of our time and focus, finishing those final tasks and last little jobs that we needed to do, we can now direct our attention to what truly matters: *love.*

Friday is a day when love and romance shine through. So, our angel of love and beauty, **Archangel Jophiel,** is here to support us. She helps us choose the most loving and high-energy words when we communicate with people, allows us to focus on loving situations, and assists us in letting go of any frustration. **Archangel Raguel** is also with us on Friday. He encourages us to release any irritations or arguments. There's no point in taking those with us into the weekend.

Raguel is also an angel who helps us with relationships, so Friday is the perfect time to pray for your soul-mate connections and your romantic partner. Whether your desire is to find or to deepen a relationship, it's a powerful idea to ask Raguel to help, affirming that each day your true love gets closer and closer to you.

Saturday

Saturday is ripe with motivation. It's the perfect day to set your goals and plan for the future. What is it that you'd like to achieve in the next 12 months? Saturday is the perfect day to think this over, as it gives you the time and the peace to really be honest about what you want.

You may wish to collect "things," to have material items around you—not because you want to show off or best your partner, but in order to be comfortable. Perhaps, for you, having more things means being more comfortable, and that in turn creates a sense of relaxation. God and your angels can speak to you much more clearly in this relaxed state. The angels know that the more at ease you are, the more willing you will be to trust your inner guidance.

On Saturday, we work with **Archangel Zadkiel,** who gives us understanding and allows us to tap into our intellect to examine the best possible scenario. **Archangel Haniel** is also with us on Saturday. Haniel is our angel of grace and wisdom. She helps us with breaking cycles and prevents us from repeating the same pattern over and over again.

Haniel inspires you to relax today, to take time out so that you can focus on peacefulness. Now you can remember what it is you want out of a situation. Are your present circumstances serving your highest good? Or is this a clever delay tactic? What is it that you want to create for yourself and your loved ones? On this day, Saturday, work to bring that into reality.

Sunday

Sunday is a day of rest, a time for you to reflect on the experiences you've had and recharge your batteries before you begin with the energy of the next week. What happened over the last six days that you can learn from? What would you change if you were faced with that same set of circumstances again? Would you do differently, or would you do it all over again?

We don't want to look back with judgment. We simply want to learn from our experiences, so that if they recur in the future, we'll know how to handle them more appropriately.

Sunday ushers in the energy of **Archangel Jeremiel,** our life-review angel who encourages us to look back on what we've already done to see any changes or alterations we may feel guided to make. On Sunday, **Archangel Ariel,** our angel of nature, helps us find time to get outdoors—to sit under a tree, perhaps, and connect with beloved animals, including pets.

As a sensitive person, you know all too well what being inside, surrounded by technological devices and artificial lighting, can do to you. Yet, when you get caught up in the momentum of the week and the many jobs you seem to be responsible for, it can feel difficult to get outside. You can see the outdoors through the window, yet it feels so distant. That's why it's so important to set aside time to feel the sunshine on your skin, to walk barefoot on the grass, to gently touch the leaves of an ancient tree and communicate with it on a deep, spiritual level. This is what true bliss is.

On Sunday, take time to rest, to reflect, and to recharge, but also to go outside. Better still, bring a notepad or journal with you so that you can jot down any inspired ideas that come to you.

Every Day

Archangel Michael is one of our strongest and loudest angels. He is created in the image of God, and his name quite literally means "He who is like God." Archangel Michael comes through with such a powerful vibration that his energy is very palpable. (Women at midlife who call upon Michael sometimes feel an intense heat wash over their bodies and mistake it for a hot flash, when in fact it is the energy of the archangel.)

This wonderful angel protects us against all fear energies. He sends away darkness and removes any blocks. Archangel Michael helps us find our life purpose and take powerful steps in the direction of our dreams. This is why we believe that Archangel Michael is guiding every single day of the week. He doesn't focus on one particular day because his energy and his essence are needed every minute.

Just as Archangel Michael watches over you, guiding you and supporting you at all times, you can work with *every* one of the archangels we've listed on *any* day of the week. By no means are you only able to call upon Archangel Jophiel on Friday and Archangel Haniel on Saturday. Rather, if you're aware of the energy and angels specifically attached to each day, you will feel more secure in your efforts to manifest your intuitive abilities.

Now you can see how starting something new on Monday might prove difficult. Doing so on Friday could also be very challenging, because it is a day centered around love and completion.

If you feel guided to change your eating patterns or other lifestyle habits, then the perfect day to initiate your efforts is Wednesday, knowing that you will have the loving support of God and all of your angels, if indeed this is what you're meant to do.

The Healing Path

The angels always say that we never really understand our true potential until we overcome the obstacle in front of us. Only then do we realize just how much strength we always had inside. We like to *think* that we know how much we can achieve, but the angels simply laugh. We really don't have any idea what we're capable of before the Universe presents us with an opportunity to rise to the occasion. It's at that moment that we redefine what we can do.

By choosing a healthy option, a more nutritious meal, you've now changed the direction of your life. God and your angels support you by making healthy food more readily available. You'll go to the supermarket and see that organic food is on special this week. You'll walk through the aisle with natural bars, nuts, and seeds, and you'll find some delicious combinations that seem like they were created just for you, with your tastes in mind. Trust your intuition and know that as you make these dietary changes, God and your angels are by your side.

You see, every single action that you take is creating a ripple effect in the Universe around you. Each step forward is an affirmation of the path you are now treading upon. When you focus on healing, you create an aura of high energy around you. Your loved ones, and the people you come into contact with—even the checker at the supermarket who helped process your grocery bill—benefit from being around your energy. Without any conscious effort, you are making a difference in someone else's day.

We love how we feel when we smile. And, yes, there are times in life when it can feel hard to summon a smile. But here's how we look at it: If we put a smile on our faces and carry on with our day, who knows how that may be helping the world. Don't you love to see people who look happy when you are out running your errands? Well, what if that person were *you?* What if *your* happiness were enough to pull others out of the darkness and make them smile themselves? It might seem simplistic, but the healing effect is extremely powerful.

With your every choice, you are creating a ripple effect of positive change. The energy from your heart opens and expands to the point where all you see is love. The angels have said that everything that comes from a place of love is healing. You will look out upon the world and see opportunities to help, to pray, to give, and to serve.

When you work with Archangel Raphael, the angel of healing, you will discover your own natural healing gifts—which can come in many different forms. It may be personal healing that you need to focus on. It may be healing through addictions and previous pain. It may be healing others with comforting touch or, perhaps, through guided words letting them know that it is safe to trust their own intuition.

When you go from someone who is simply *being*—someone who is only sitting and thinking—to someone who is *doing,* who's taking action, that's when the real miracle begins. Please understand that no matter how small or large that first step may be, you are creating positive changes all around you.

AFTERWORD

To You and Your Health,
with Love and Light

We are all highly intuitive beings once we bring our focus back to natural, high-vibrational foods. Changing the way we eat really *can* change the way we see the world.

Allow opportunities to come your way with ease. Release drama, stress, and all kinds of tension by knowing that you are being led along a path of joy.

Be confident in making choices that are right for you, as they also benefit others. Spend time doing the things you love. You are far more inspirational when each action you take is filled with joy.

Please realize that when certain issues are important to you, but other people don't seem to notice them, it shows that they're a part of your spiritual purpose. Don't try to change your beliefs or become apathetic, where you no longer care what happens. Instead, you need to take a stand, to speak up and tell everybody else what you're feeling. Have the courage to be a heavenly spotlight, illuminating something that the rest of us may be in the dark about.

By coming to Earth with this particular purpose, you will help others realize the importance of that mission. So we thank you for having the courage to see it through.

We know that by making some conscious nutritional adjustments, you will enhance your intuition and receive guidance about your individual life purpose. We encourage you to practice regular meditation to allow yourself to connect with your Higher Self on a deeper level. Even just a few minutes of quiet solitude can deliver profound insights.

May you always recognize and trust the Divine guidance you receive.

Many blessings,
Doreen and Robert

APPENDIX

"Clair" Food Chart

Clairvoyance

Enjoy	Avoid
Sun-ripened organic fruits such as pineapple	Caffeine
Dark leafy greens	Alcohol
Broccoli	Fluoride (because it calcifies the pineal gland and reduces clairvoyance)
Coconut	
Mango	
Grapefruit	
Kale	
Watermelon	
Blueberries	
Strawberries	
Spinach	

Clairsentience

Enjoy	Avoid
Beans and other legumes	Animal fats
Broccoli	Fried foods
Cauliflower	Refined sugar
Cabbage	Alcohol
Organic nuts	Saturated fats
Sea vegetables	Cigarette smoke
Squash	Chemicals
Carrots	Foods containing lectin (uncooked legumes such as beans/pulses—well cooked is fine)
Yams	
Beets	Spicy foods
Raspberries	Caffeine
Sweet potatoes	Chemical additives
Red peppers	Genetically modified organisms (GMOs)
Tomatoes	
Cantaloupe	Dairy products
Papaya	
Dark leafy greens	
Sunflower seeds	
Pistachio nuts	
Bananas	
Avocado	
Spinach	
Kale	
Asparagus	
Oranges	

Clairaudience

Enjoy	Avoid
Flaxseeds or flaxseed oil	Fried foods
Nuts	Cigarette smoke
Broccoli	Loud noises
Green leafy vegetables	
Citrus fruits	
Beans	
Peas	
Lentils	
Avocados	
Brussels sprouts	
Seeds	
Celery	
Carrots	
Squash	
Corn	
Cauliflower	
Rice	
Bananas	
Potatoes	
Pomegranates	

Claircognizance

Enjoy	Avoid
Breakfast each morning for better cognitive performance	Caffeine
Walnuts	Refined sugar
Pumpkin seeds	Alcohol
Flaxseeds	Gluten
Beans	
Cabbage	
Broccoli	
Cauliflower	
Blueberries	
Chia seeds	
Ginger	
Celery	

Healing Insights for Each Chakra

Root Chakra
Location: Base of your spine
Color: Red
Musical Note: C
Crystals: Red Jasper, garnet, hematite
Flowers: Carnation, daisy, tulip
Affirmation: I am safe and protected. All of my earthly needs are met and provided for.
Activity: Walk barefoot in the grass.
Foods: Potato, squash, pumpkin, beets, raspberries

Sacral Chakra
Location: One inch below your navel
Color: Orange
Musical Note: D
Crystals: Carnelian, labradorite
Flowers: Banksia, fuchsia, gerbera
Affirmation: I express my creativity with ease. My desires are balanced by my current commitments.
Activity: Work on something artistic.
Foods: Carrot, tomato, watercress, Almond Mylk, cantaloupe, papaya

Solar-Plexus Chakra
Location: Stomach area just under your sternum
Color: Yellow
Musical Note: E
Crystals: Citrine, pyrite
Flowers: Bluebell, yellow lily, yellow rose
Affirmation: It is safe for me to be powerful. I am confident in all that I do.
Activity: Try something that you normally wouldn't try. Push yourself a little out of your comfort zone.
Foods: Organic, non-GMO tofu, lemon, Sunflower Mylk, mango

Heart Chakra

Location: Center of the chest

Color: Emerald green with sparkles of pink

Musical Note: F

Crystals: Rose quartz, aventurine, malachite

Flowers: Chrysanthemum, orchid, red rose

Affirmation: It is safe for me to love. I easily express love. I easily receive love.

Activities: Tell someone your true feelings. Watch a romantic movie. Write a touching letter of thanks or gratitude to someone who's helped you.

Foods: Kale, apple, watermelon, spinach

Throat Chakra

Location: Throat area/Adam's apple

Color: Sky blue

Musical Note: G

Crystals: Blue lace agate, sodalite, kyanite

Flowers: Daffodil, snapdragon

Affirmation: I speak with loving confidence. My words help others to heal. It is safe for me to communicate and share what's in my heart.

Activities: Try singing while you're alone. Call a dear friend and chat in a supportive and mutually beneficial way.

Foods: Cucumber, garlic, Cashew Mylk, strawberries

Ear Chakras

Location: Above each of your eyebrows

Color: Violet red

Musical Note: A #

Crystals: Ametrine, rutilated quartz

Flowers: Bird-of-paradise

Affirmation: All that I hear brings me peace.

Activity: Listen to meditation music or singing bowls.

Foods: Ginger, pomegranate

Third-Eye Chakra

Location: Between your eyebrows

Color: Dark blue with sparkles of purple

Musical Note: A

Crystals: Amethyst, celestite

Flowers: Echinacea, lavender, pansy

Affirmation: It is safe for me to be intuitive. I trust my visions and insights.

Activities: Give yourself, or a friend, an oracle-card reading. Read a spiritual book. Work with crystals.

Foods: Pineapple, celery, broccoli, blueberries, acai, coconut

Crown Chakra

Location: Top of the head

Color: Purple with sparkles of white

Musical Note: B

Crystals: Fluorite, clear quartz, selenite, apophyllite

Flowers: Lotus, white rose, African violet

Affirmation: I am Divinely guided by God.

Activities: Meditate. Watch the sunrise.

Foods: Grapes, blueberries, Macadamia Mylk, banana, pear, grapefruit

Spiritual Applications of Nutritional Supplements

Vitamins

Vitamin A

Vitamin A is a strong antioxidant as well as a powerful healer. It helps us mount a healthy response to allergens. When pollen or dust enters our system, the immune system wants to remove this foreign body. Some people have an exaggerated response and instantly start sneezing and coughing, mucus pours out of their noses, their eyes become red and itchy, and they develop a scratchy throat. These are all ways that our bodies try to push out pathogens, but some people are much more sensitive.

Vitamin A helps balance this reaction. When a foreign body such as dust or pollen comes into contact with you, your system can clear it out through less severe means. Vitamin A helps break down mucus congestion while also removing the irritating agent.

Vitamin A heals any kind of cut or superficial wound that you may have. It binds tissues together perfectly, reducing scarring and combating infection. It helps clear your skin of acne, too, as it heals the site of infection.

In addition to balancing your immune system, it also helps heal your vision and has an affinity for the eyes. If you have trouble seeing at nighttime, you may have a vitamin A deficiency.

Vitamin A is a fat-soluble nutrient, so it's important to recognize that you don't want to take this supplement long-term. It will be stored in your body for some time. Vitamin A is best taken for short periods (up to three months), followed by a break.

When you take vitamin A in supplemental form, you may aim for between 5,000 and 15,000 International Units (IU) daily. Take this divided throughout the day—for example, 5,000 IU three times a day as a maximum.

Energetically, this nutrient helps change our perspective on how others perceive us. We all have this idea of how other people view us. What they see when they look at us is different from how we see ourselves in the mirror. The ego voice will tell us one thing, when the reality is very different—and often much more positive.

If we go out into the world feeling withdrawn and shy because we feel that people are judging us, others are looking upon us negatively, or we're the target of attack, our experience is going to be clouded. If, instead, we're able to open up our hearts and allow our love to shine through, we can change the way other people see us—or, at least, *our* perception of what they see.

B Vitamins

B vitamins—involved in so many different reactions throughout your precious body—are the key nutrients that help regulate your mood and appetite. Just to think a single thought, you are using B_6, B_9, and B_{12}. Every mental task, every memory you create, is reliant on B vitamins.

You may not have considered before that the process of thinking and becoming consciously aware could use up nutrients. Well, it does—but that doesn't mean you have to be concerned about it. If you live a healthy, nutrition-filled lifestyle, there's nothing to worry about! So many wonderful natural foods are rich in B vitamins.

B vitamins help balance our moods, allowing us to feel energized and happy. That's why they're also excellent for reducing feelings of anxiety.

When we're stressed, everything goes much, much faster. We feel like we're running out of time, and the ego voice jumps in to tell us that we have a limited supply of what we need. The B vitamins get us back on track again—get us to slow down and take a breath. They help us focus and clear our minds of any unwanted thoughts so we can think clearly and understand new topics.

B vitamins are also key in carbohydrate digestion. When the body is processing and absorbing carbohydrates, if we have enough B vitamins, we'll break those carbs down and use them as energy. If we don't have enough, then our bodies will convert those carbohydrates to fat cells and store them for later use. If you feel like you're craving sugary things or lots of breads, then think about taking some B vitamins, as that may be the answer for you.

B vitamins are truly wonderful healers, performing many vital reactions throughout your body. They even help in the formation and maintenance of red blood cells. They keep you healthy on a cellular level.

If you choose to supplement, select a natural, organic brand that has a broad spectrum of the different B vitamins. Make sure, as well, that the formula is balanced, with adequate amounts of each nutrient rather than loads of one and just small amounts of the others. Unbalanced formulas can actually lead to B vitamin deficiencies. Of course, if in doubt, check with your health-care professional or naturopath.

B vitamins help us to hear the voice of our intuition much more clearly. They dissolve the voice of fear that can sometimes become overwhelming. If we listen to our angels, they teach us to see the positivity within all of us. This allows us to see that the worst is not in front of us, but instead the future is a wonderful opportunity to test our strength.

When you take B vitamins, it clears your mind of those limiting, self-deprecating thoughts and leaves a sense of peace.

Vitamin C

Most people will reach for vitamin C at the first sign of a cold or flu, and quite rightly so. But what else can this powerful nutrient do for us?

Well, it's a wonderful antioxidant, helping protect you from any kind of oxidative damage. This means it detoxifies your body of free radicals. As an example, think of a rusted piece of metal. The metal was once shiny and strong, but through the attack of free radicals and oxidative damage, it rusted and became brittle. Vitamin C helps your body to be strong, and prevents this kind of damage from occurring.

Free radicals can affect us through environmental pollution and toxins. They can come through dietary habits, also. As we age, our cells also age and can become more susceptible to free radicals and oxidative stress. The more antioxidants your body has, the more protected every cell is going to be.

Diseases such as cancer arise when the cell is reproduced incorrectly. The cell looks misshapen, but it continues to replicate itself. The vitamin C helps protect your cells from any kind of damage so that as they reproduce, they remain healthy. It also maintains the production of good-quality blood cells.

Vitamin C supports collagen synthesis, which means it helps tone your skin. The breakdown of collagen is what leads to wrinkles. Collagen gives your skin elasticity. Vitamin C is wonderful for healing wounds and preventing scarring. You may see vitamin C–enriched skin lotions in the cosmetic section of your department store. That's because when vitamin C is absorbed into your skin, it helps repair damage and also produces youthful, elastic skin. It allows collagen to be synthesized, which helps smooth out any wrinkles and repair scars.

Vitamin C can even help detoxify your body from chemicals and heavy metals. It has an affinity for lead, capturing it, binding to it, and dragging it out of your bloodstream.

Vitamin C helps recharge your adrenal glands and gives your body the fuel it needs to keep going. Think of this like the hybrid power for the motor of your body. As you go through your daily processes, you're using up precious fuel. That's the way your body has been designed. Then, as you rest in the evening, your body recharges itself. Over time, if you become particularly stressed, if you have long, extended workdays and you struggle to sleep, then your "battery pack" (your adrenal glands) starts to be depleted. Vitamin C helps refill the fuel tank and restore your energy reserves so that you can continue pressing forward.

It's a beautifully healing nutrient. It heals any tissue damage and also helps heal through infection, but it only does so at the correct dosage. If there is any sign of infection, you need to make sure you're taking enough vitamin C. So many people will take 500 or even 1,000 milligrams (mg) and think that they're doing their body wonderful service to protect against the infection. However, you may need to go as high as 10,000 mg per day in order to fight off that infection. To take 10,000 mg as a supplement is going to be somewhat difficult. In some hospitals and doctors' clinics, they will give you vitamin C as an intravenous process.

To ensure that you are taking enough vitamin C to heal your body, you want to make sure that the supplement is high quality. Many people think that vitamin C is extracted from oranges, but did you know that the majority comes from corn? Unfortunately, corn is highly genetically modified in much of the world, so we need to make sure that the vitamin C we're taking comes from non-GMO sources and is ideally organic.

I (Robert) prefer to take vitamin C that is a combination of mineral ascorbates. Ascorbic acid is the most absorbable form of vitamin C, but if you take it in high amounts, it can cause digestive upsets and a generally acidic feeling in your stomach. So it's better balanced when you take it with mineral ascorbates, such as calcium ascorbate, sodium ascorbate, and the like. You'll see this listed on the label right there with the ascorbic acid. Sometimes, these types of products are labeled *buffered vitamin C*.

If you're feeling guided to take vitamin C, do so in divided doses. It works best when you take smaller amounts more frequently, rather than a large amount all at once. Try for 1,500 to 2,000 mg two or three times a day. It won't do you any good if you take 5,000 mg in one big dose—it's just going to go straight through you.

On an energetic level, vitamin C helps shield your aura. If you're in areas where people speak negatively, vitamin C can protect you so that you don't take on board any of that fear-based energy. It also helps when you're around people who have harsh energy or in environments that feel dark and repressed, allowing you to rise above any confusion and chaos to let the world hear your voice. What is it that you have to say? Start sharing this message now.

As you can see, vitamin C does so many wonderful healing things throughout the body. It's perhaps no surprise that Archangel Raphael is strongly connected to this nutrient. Together, Raphael and vitamin C help your body heal on a deep, cellular level. This healing duo invigorates you, giving you the confidence to follow through with your purpose and the courage to take the next step on your journey, press forward, and never back down.

Don't allow anybody to extinguish your flame of positivity. And if the darkness does overcome you, it just means you have to shine even more brightly. As you take vitamin C, your energy will radiate outward, casting away the darkness. After all, there's nothing that the darkness fears more than the shining light of love.

Allow yourself to be all that you are meant to be. Have the courage to stand up and speak your Divine truth. Know that you're protected, that you're being healed, and that you're also being a healing inspiration to those around you. Every word you speak and every action you take is creating a cascade of healing energy around you. The people you interact with benefit from what you have to share. You, just by being a comforting person to speak with, can do a tremendous amount of good in somebody else's world.

Vitamin D

Vitamin D is something your body can naturally produce from the healing rays of the sun. However, people all over the world are deficient in vitamin D. For example, tremendous numbers of Australians have vitamin D deficiencies. Many feel this is a side effect of the information campaign warning against the harmful effects of the sun.

In Australia, there is a high rate of skin cancer due to the UV radiation that damages the cells of the skin. A lot of money and time was invested into teaching people to stay out of the harsh rays to protect them from getting skin cancer. Unfortunately, many people became so afraid that they avoided the sun altogether, only going outdoors if they were completely covered or wearing sunscreen all over their bodies. This blocked the ability of their bodies to create vitamin D.

Your body needs unfiltered sunlight in order for vitamin D synthesis to take place. The sun's rays can't go through clothing, sunscreen, or glass. There has to be direct contact between the sun and your skin. Of course, you need to practice safe sun exposure and do so at the hours when the light is not at its harshest. Go outside in the early morning and late afternoon when the sun is warm and beautiful. It's energizing and uplifting rather than burning and damaging.

The angels have taught us that as you watch the sun rising in the morning, your chakras are opened and awakened. This invigorates you for the day ahead. As you experience the sun setting in the evening, it clears your energy from the day and prepares you for a restful night of sleep.

This recent sun phobia led to our needing vitamin D supplementation, and you may also feel guided to take vitamin D from time to time. Many jobs involve being indoors, under artificial lighting for the majority of the day. With our increasingly technological society, many people are spending their free time inside playing with their gadgets. So it may be necessary to look at spending more time outdoors as well as supplementing with vitamin D periodically to make sure your body has enough of what it needs. I (Robert) encourage my patients to consider supplementation once every three to six months.

We used to think that vitamin D was mostly important for bone health. After all, vitamin D helps strengthen the bones and places the calcium where it's needed so bones stay strong and healthy. We'd only focus on osteoporosis patients, and encourage them to be more aware of their vitamin D intake. However, through recent research, it has been found that vitamin D is valuable for so much more than just strong bones. It's been used in various studies and research trials, including treatment of eczema in children. One of the most amazing things that vitamin D can do is to help stop the growth of cancer cells, checking each cell being reproduced to ensure it looks the way it's meant to; if there's any kind of damage or the cell is replicating itself too quickly, then the vitamin D will slow it down.

It is interesting that vitamin D slows down the growth of cancer, while at the same time the sun can *create* cancer through damaging UV rays. We asked the angels about this, and here's what they had to say: People who need to be outdoors all day long seem to rarely get sunburned. These people's bodies have become used to the energy from the sun, and for them it's not unusual to be outside in the heat of the day. On the other hand, when somebody who mostly stays indoors or in shaded areas then goes out at high noon, their bodies don't know how to handle the sun. Their skin burns and becomes damaged because it is unused to such intense rays.

If you are a person who spends most of the time inside an office, then start taking five- to ten-minute breaks outside during the day. Doing so will help your body adjust to being in the sun. That way, if you do go on vacation and happen to find yourself out in the strongest rays, your body won't sustain as much damage. Instead, it will receive the vitamin D it needs, which will help slow down cellular damage.

Your body also needs certain nutrients to allow the conversion of sunlight into vitamin D. If your nutritional intake is insufficient, then you may need to supplement. The body has a wonderful intelligence; we just need to provide it with proper fuel in order to allow those healing processes to take place. Vitamin D balances our immune system and is a good support for allergy responses.

Vitamin D also promotes the development of nerve growth factor. Medically, it was believed that nerves would never regrow. If a nerve received any kind of damage, then that was it—full stop, end of sentence, nothing would change. Through recent research, however, it was found that while nerve cells may not be able to regenerate, the body is smart enough to create new pathways around the damaged area. There are accounts of stroke victims regaining function, even after being half-paralyzed. Some people lost the ability to control one of their arms or several of their fingers, but over time their mobility improved as their bodies produced new nerve growth factors and created a new pathway around the damaged piece. They started to use that arm again, or those fingers, and it was like nothing had ever happened.

In an effort to remove most toxins from your life, we suggest avoiding lanolin-based vitamin D products. Lanolin is a substance that sheep secrete into their wool. If the sheep are not eating an organic diet, then they'll be excreting toxins and chemicals through their skin and into this lanolin. The vitamin D is extracted from the lanolin, encapsulated, and sold as a supplement for you to consume.

It is unfortunate that most vitamin D supplements are extracted from lanolin, and most companies do not label this on the bottles.

Another major source of vitamin D is cod liver oil (which is also rich in vitamin A). However, through overharvesting, we are now damaging the ecosystems of the ocean. A better solution is to get good-quality, vegan vitamin D from plant sources such as seaweed. After all, those fish that are so rich in vitamin D feed off seaweed. The seaweed is converting the energy from the sun into vitamin D.

As a general maintenance dose, you may only need 400 IU. But if there's a deficiency that's become apparent through a blood test, then you may need to take 2,000 IU for two to three months. Of course, check with your health-care professional to make sure that this is right for you.

Energetically, vitamin D helps make you strong, confident, and courageous. It allows you to stand tall and be the authentic version of who you're meant to be. Remember that God and the angels have not made any mistakes in your creation. The way you are right now is the way that you are meant to be.

Emotionally, vitamin D helps you hear another perspective. This is why we think it's a good idea to take a course of vitamin D every three to six months. It allows you to have an objective look at how you're handling things and ask yourself honestly, "Is this the best way?" Just because you've done something for a long time doesn't mean it's the most efficient or the healthiest way. So listen to the advice of those people around you. Take a look at your surroundings and really give yourself permission and courage to make changes where you need to.

Vitamin E

Vitamin E is an antioxidant, but what makes it particularly special is its effect inside the cell. Unlike vitamin C, which helps protect your body from oxidative damage in general, vitamin E very specifically targets the inside of your cells. This makes it excellent for people with a long history of unhealthy eating habits.

Visualize a perfect, pure cell suspended in your body. If you eat the occasional unhealthy item, any toxins will float through your bloodstream and, for the most part, bypass your pure cell. However, if you were to continually eat unhealthy foods, those toxins would be floating through your bloodstream more often. This means that your perfect little cell is exposed to more damaging material. Over time the cell begins to absorb toxins from its surroundings. Vitamin E gets inside your cells and prevents further damage from occurring.

Vitamin E is wonderful for heart health. It facilitates blood flow throughout the body. It can even help break down, and remove, excess cholesterol. Vitamin E reduces inflammation throughout your entire body, while particularly resonating with the heart area, healing your cardiovascular system.

On an energetic level, vitamin E helps mend a broken heart. If you feel used and abused, taken advantage of, or even just fragile, vitamin E heals that past pain and allows your heart to shine with love once more.

You don't have to take much vitamin E to have this effect, either: between 200 and 800 IU per day (you can try as little as 200 IU once daily, or 200 to 400 IU twice a day).

As your heart begins to mend, your body will also heal from the inside out. It's like clearing away a stain on the carpet. If we just do a superficial, surface cleaning, over time that old stain reappears. It can look like we never did any of the work to begin with. But if we take that extra effort and really get down to the deeper layers, then we remove the stain at its source and it can never come back.

When you feel guided to work with vitamin E, it balances your cholesterol levels, heals inflammation, and provides antioxidant protection. Energetically, it is healing your heart so that you can love again. You'll be bringing compassion and joy back into your life.

Minerals

Calcium

Calcium is important for bone formation. It helps keep your skeletal system strong, yet also flexible. When bones become deficient in calcium, people are diagnosed as osteoporotic, and their bones become brittle and fragile. When your body has enough calcium, there's no need for you to worry about deficiencies in your skeleton.

Something that can create a deficiency that you may not have considered is drinking large amounts of soda. Most fizzy beverages contain carbonic acid, which leaches calcium out of your bones and makes it difficult for your body to remineralize them again. These drinks essentially weaken your bone structure.

Calcium is also important for muscle contraction. It has a symbiotic connection with magnesium; together, they allow your muscles to contract and relax at the appropriate times.

When you experience the sensation of pain, the message is received through the nerve fiber and sent back up into the brain. However, if your body is lacking adequate amounts of calcium, then the nerve conducts its message erratically and makes the pain feel much more intense than it should. Calcium helps your nerves send messages along their fibers more effectively. By consuming foods rich in calcium, you can have a better pain tolerance. Your muscles will relax and your skeleton will remain strong.

Many think that the best source of calcium is from dairy products, yet commercial milk comes from animals that are entirely unlike humans. When you consume dairy products, your body doesn't really know how to handle this foreign substance. It doesn't digest it properly, and this often leads to inflammation.

Sesame seeds are a rich source of calcium. By weight, they are one of the foods highest in calcium that we have available. You can enjoy tahini, which is a spread made out of sesame seeds, in salad dressings or served as a sauce. Other foods rich in calcium are broccoli, almonds, spinach, seaweed, and mustard greens.

If you are deficient in calcium, you may need up to 2,000 mg per day. If you're supplementing for general maintenance, then you may only need 1,000 mg. Most supplements are made of calcium carbonate, which is quite difficult for your body to absorb. Try including calcium-rich foods at each meal to ensure your body is getting natural, absorbable calcium.

Energetically, calcium gives us an emotional backbone. It provides us with the stability and the confidence to be who we are in truth. No longer do we have to worry about what other people think of us. Instead, we choose to stand tall and strong, knowing that we are in the perfect place at the perfect time.

Iron

Iron helps with the production of healthy blood. It also plays a role in growth and development, whether that be through infancy, during adolescence, or even in adulthood. We're constantly growing, and each cell is going to be replaced with a different one within a few years. Every red blood cell is repaired and recycled every three or four months, and iron is integral to this process.

When you have abundant iron throughout your system, you have a healthy immune system. You feel energetic. You feel inspired. You feel ready for the next step.

On an energetic level, iron helps you stay strong. It grants you unwavering faith in your beliefs. If other people challenge your belief in angels, iron helps you stand firm in those moments. It allows you to hear what the other person is saying, while you hold on to your cherished core values.

Before you take iron supplements, we strongly suggest having a blood test. While this may seem uncomfortable, it is the best way to ensure your safety. Taking too much iron for too long damages your body. It is a nutrient stored in your tissues, so it isn't something you should supplement with very often if you don't need it.

If you lack sufficient iron or are on the lower end of the scale, then you may consider supplementation. Aim for a dosage between 20 and 40 mg per day. Most pharmaceutical iron supplements contain ten times this dose because they use iron that is poorly absorbed; this sometimes leads to unwanted side effects. Health-food stores have natural iron supplements, which are lower in dosage but are better tolerated by the body.

Magnesium

Magnesium is a recommended mineral for those who exercise a lot. However, it's also very important for those who do not exercise at all—and, of course, it's beneficial for people in between. Every time your muscles contract, your body is releasing magnesium. Constant muscle contractions use up the magnesium within your body. When magnesium enters your body, it helps relax your muscles and joints, allowing you to feel comfortable.

Tired muscles slow down the flow of blood. Metabolites and lactic acid build up in your system, which is why you feel sore and achy after a hard workout. Magnesium balances your muscles so that fresh blood flow whisks away the painful buildup.

Magnesium helps your body achieve a sense of relaxation, not only from the muscles but also throughout your nervous system. It won't put you to sleep or make you drowsy; it just relaxes your nervous system enough that you can go to sleep when you need to. If you're somebody who goes to bed every evening and lies there for an hour or two feeling restless, tossing and turning with an overactive mind, then you will absolutely love magnesium.

You'll want to aim for between 400 and 800 mg of magnesium per day. We've found that magnesium reaches its peak absorbency approximately seven hours after you take it. If you wake up feeling achy and sore, or fatigued and stressed, then take magnesium before bed, so you'll have about seven hours for this mineral to fully charge you. If you have trouble sleeping, then take the magnesium in the morning or afternoon. As evening approaches, your body already has enough absorbed magnesium to promote relaxation.

Magnesium can be useful if you have trouble meditating for long periods of time. If you feel fidgety and restless, try magnesium. A relaxed body and nervous system allows you to sit in quiet solitude and tune in to your intuitive guidance.

Selenium

Selenium is another antioxidant that supports your body. It's a powerful mineral that requires you to exercise some caution. Almost every bottle will have a label warning that it's a toxic element that can cause harm at high doses. While this is true, the difficulty comes when no one can seem to agree on what a "high dose" is. Some experts say 200 mcg is the most you should take, yet other practitioners have safely prescribed 600 mcg to patients. The reason for the confusion is that selenium can be taken in higher amounts *only* if your body needs it. If you're relatively healthy, then 600 mcg is way too much for you. We recommend erring on the side of caution and taking only 50 mcg per day unless you get professional supervision. Garlic is a good dietary source of selenium.

Selenium helps your body to detox and promotes clearing of toxic compounds. This is why it is often used in cancer treatments, since it also has anti-tumor properties.

Everything has an energetic healing property, yet when we meditated on selenium we found something interesting. This nutrient seems to have a language all its own! It's unlike anything else we've meditated upon or asked the angels about. It seems to have its own intelligence but also a very deep and kind of perplexing nature. We suspect this may be why it's also confused practitioners and researchers in the past. Our guidance says that selenium isn't something to take for extended periods of time (no longer than three months). When you take it, you will learn a great deal about yourself. You'll understand more about why you react to situations in a certain way, but the journey could be intense.

Zinc

Zinc is such an overachieving nutrient. It doesn't necessarily create healing miracles by itself. Instead, it helps facilitate hundreds of reactions within your body. (We like to think of it as the "taxi" mineral; it's the vehicle that takes us from point A to point B.) Medical science has documented at least 400 different metabolic processes that zinc is required for. Quite simply, if you do not get enough zinc, then there are at least 400 reactions that your body is going to struggle to complete.

Zinc is important for your brain. It helps balance your moods and hormones. It uplifts your soul and shows you a bright, cheerful outlook. When you are accustomed to seeing chaos in the world, zinc sheds light on the higher purpose. When people feel depressed, lethargic, and tired, zinc can help refuel their system. It brings back inspiration so that they can move forward with love.

One of the many functions that zinc is involved in is suppressing tumors. Zinc helps activate tumor-suppressing factors. As these float throughout your bloodstream, they slow down and inhibit the production of malignant cells.

Interestingly, zinc is important for sensory functions such as taste. Think of children who are considered fussy eaters, just picking at their meals and not eating a great deal. It seems their taste for different foods changes from week to week. Often this points to a zinc deficiency! When you're low in zinc, it affects your ability to taste. Your taste buds actually change and can no longer receive flavors such as sweetness, saltiness, or sourness. If you feel that your child or another loved one is deficient in zinc, please check with a health-care provider for the best dosage and type of zinc for them.

Zinc also affects our sense of smell. If you inhale the scent of a beautiful, delicate rose, the fragrance will emanate through your soul and uplift you in unimaginable ways. However, if you are low on zinc, then you may not receive all of the benefits that the aroma has to offer.

Zinc is important for your immune system, with wonderful antiviral properties. It boosts your body's defenses and protects you from any pathogens. It helps protect your skin and promotes healthy skin tissue and healing. Zinc is also a beneficial aid in reproductive issues for both men and women.

Take between 30 and 60 mg per day in a supplemental form. It is a heavier mineral, which means that if you take it with other medications or even other supplements, it may interact with them. Although it's uncommon for those interactions to cause side effects, it will often prevent proper absorption. This can delay, or reduce, the effect of medications. Zinc pushes everything else out of the way so that it gets first priority. If you are on prescription medications, take them and the zinc at least two hours apart.

On an energetic and emotional level, zinc helps us achieve the many tasks around us. It's perfect for spiritual healers and psychics who feel overwhelmed by their current workload. It's great for people who feel like they're jumping from one task to another and not quite getting on top of everything. If you feel like your energy is being spread too thin, the guidance you're getting from God and your angels is to slow down. It may be necessary to take a moment to rest and recharge, then focus your intentions on only one or two activities at a time. When you finish those activities, you can move on to the next one. This approach allows you to feel relaxed and peaceful, and to complete that powerful work in a healthy and balanced way.

We don't need lightworkers to be burned-out—we need the exact opposite! We need you to be inspired. We need you to have your intuition switched on, turned up full volume, so that you can receive all of the magical messages from the Divine.

Taking zinc also improves your confidence. This allows you to stand in your power and trust that you're going in the right direction, right now. Don't fear that you've taken an alternative avenue to reach your life purpose and your destiny. The zinc will soon remind you that you are exactly where you are meant to be and everything is going according to plan.

Other Supplements

Coenzyme Q10

Coenzyme Q10 (or CoQ10) is an excellent antioxidant. It clears through cholesterol, helping heal your heart and reduce high blood pressure.

CoQ10 can be thought of as the spark plug for the body. It gives your metabolism, and your body in general, a real surge of energy. This isn't an artificial energy like caffeine or sugar. Instead, CoQ10 unlocks the energetic potential that's already available to you within your cells. It breaks down stored fat, which allows your body to use it as energy. It flicks a switch that tells your body to start healing, start using those energy reserves, and start thinking more clearly and positively.

When you take this supplement, it helps you feel a momentum starting to build. On an energetic and spiritual level, CoQ10 helps you press forward even when you might be afraid. You may feel scared or think that an idea could fail, but the CoQ10 will give you the courage to push past the fear and go with that surge of creative, inspired, motivated energy. It shows you that nothing is impossible; in fact, all of your dreams can come true if you allow them to. Don't stand in the way of your amazing future.

There's nothing that you can't achieve. CoQ10 offers the reassurance that you can do anything and the courage to take the first step.

Dosages for CoQ10 can range between 100 and 500 mg. Now, this is a more expensive supplement, but inexpensive brands tend to be of poor quality and contain synthetic products rather than the real coenzyme. So please ensure that you get good-quality, high-strength CoQ10 rather than cheaper versions.

Essential Fatty Acids and Healthy Oils

There are two main groups of healthy omega oils that we look at: omega-3 and omega-6. Fish oils contain omega-3, which has beneficial properties for inflammation as well as brain health. Omega-6 also offers nervous-system support as well as some anti-inflammatory properties. Your body does not produce these on its own—which is why they're also called *essential fatty acids* (EFAs)—so you need to get them from a dietary source.

The most common source for the fatty acids in supplements is fish. There are issues regarding the quality and the integrity of the fish oil, plus concerns about overharvesting. You can go to your local health-food store or supermarket and find fish-oil supplements very inexpensively, perhaps $15 for over 100 capsules. However, most of the time this fish oil is not going to be beneficial to your body. The processes used to create those capsules often cause the oil inside to go rancid. This leads to oxidative damage within your body rather than healing.

We prefer vegetarian options and enjoy flaxseed oil since it contains a combination of omega-3 and omega-6 fatty acids. It's an abundant, plant-based source of fatty acids. You can take flaxseed oil as a liquid or a capsule, and you can also include whole or ground flaxseeds in your smoothies or breakfast cereals.

When you're consuming these beautiful essential fatty acids, they'll help heal any kind of painful inflammation in your body and remove harmful metabolites from your bloodstream. They also balance your nervous system, uplifting your mood by giving your brain the nourishment it needs. They can help you sleep and are particularly useful if you have difficulty staying asleep. If you wake up every few hours, then you may be deficient in essential fatty acids.

These healing oils protect the cell membranes that create the structure of your blood cells. This is very important because when the membrane around those cells is healthy, it allows beneficial nutrients to be absorbed and to be sent out.

These oils are also healthy for the heart. They aid in regulating cholesterol and blood pressure.

Aim for around 3,000 mg of essential fatty acids per day. If you're taking flaxseed oil capsules, then a divided dose of 1,500 mg twice a day is appropriate. If you're enjoying flaxseed oil as a food, then usually a tablespoon or so is enough to give you all of the essential fatty acids your body needs.

Energetically, the essential fatty acids are nurturing, like a comforting hug that wraps around your body. Essential fatty acids bring you a sense of fulfillment. They take away a feeling of emptiness and lack. They allow you to feel content with everything around you at this point. They remind you that you are always being provided for and not a moment has gone by in the history of your life where you haven't been perfectly taken care of. Trust that every moment from this point will hold the same truth. You will be protected, you will be provided for, and you will be safe.

SAMe

SAMe (pronounced sam-ee) is a highly effective supplement that aids in pain relief, detoxification, and mood elevation. I (Robert) love using SAMe because I have seen its healing effects time and time again. When you feel down and depressed, SAMe very quickly pulls you up and brings back joy. Some products just treat symptoms and ignore the true cause, but SAMe clears away the darkness and reveals your unwavering joy.

I'm a happy person the majority of the time, but I like to try different supplements before I feel comfortable recommending them to patients or writing about them. When I took some SAMe, within a few days I felt even more joyful and loving than usual! It helped open me up to more laughter that came from within. This is how I find SAMe to be the most effective—bringing more light, love, and joy into someone's soul. Yes, it also helps with pain management and can clear toxins out of your bloodstream, but nothing can lift your spirits like SAMe can.

For best results, it's important to take enough. Aim for between 400 and 1,200 mg. Generally, I will start people on 800 mg and see how they fare.

Choose a good-quality product that will give you high levels of SAMe. It may contain a few other nutrients to help its absorption, such as zinc and B vitamins. The trick is getting a good balance so that you don't overdo the other nutrients. A product I use and find highly effective has the following formula:

- S-Adenosyl-methionine disuphate tosylate—873.6 mg (equivalent to S-Adenosyl-methionine [SAMe]—400 mg)

- Cyanocobalamin (B_{12})—1 mg

- Riboflavin (B_2)—20 mg

- Zinc amino acid chelate—50 mg (equivalent zinc—10 mg)

- Folic acid (B_9)—90 mcg

- Pyridoxine hydrochloride—50 mg (equivalent pyridoxine [B_6]—41.15 mg)

Unfortunately, SAMe is a little more costly than other supplements. This is because it's an unstable compound, so there are extra steps involved in its production that we, as consumers, then pay for. However, it really is worth the investment if you feel guided to use it.

Energetically, SAMe brings light to your spirit by clearing away any clouds of darkness. If you focus on negativity, you attract more of it. The more negativity around you, the harder and harder it becomes to see the light. This product helps you find the tiny glimmer of hope and capture it. Your attention is pulled to the positive and thus you attract more positivity. It builds its own momentum and soon you are surrounded by healing, uplifting, positive energy!

BIBLIOGRAPHY

Age-Related Eye Disease Study Research Group. (2001). A randomized, placebo-controlled, clinical trial of high-dose supplementation with vitamins C and E, beta carotene, and zinc for age-related macular degeneration and vision loss: AREDS report no. 8. *Arch Ophthalmol,* 119(10), 1417–36.

Ayyadurai, VA, & Deonikar, P. (2015, Jul). Do GMOs accumulate formaldehyde and disrupt molecular systems equilibria? Systems biology may provide answers. *Agricultural Sciences,* 6, 630–62. Retrieved from http://www.scirp.org/journal/PaperInformation .aspx?PaperID=57871

Bargh, JA. (1996, Jan). The automatic evaluation effect: Unconditional automatic attitude activation with a pronunciation task. *Journal of Experimental Social Psychology,* 32(1), 104–28.

Biesalski, HK, Wellner, U, & Weiser, H. (1990). Vitamin A deficiency increases noise susceptibility in guinea pigs. *J. Nutr.,* 120(7), 726–37.

Bone, K. (2003). *A Clinical Guide to Blending Liquid Herbs.* St. Louis, MO: Churchill Livingstone.

Chandra, RK. (1981). Single nutrient deficiency and cell-mediated immune responses. II. Pyridoxine. *Nutrition Research,* 1(1), 101–6.

Cherednichenko, G, et al. (2012, Aug 28). Triclosan impairs excitation–contraction coupling and Ca2+ dynamics in striated muscle. *Proc Natl Acad Sci USA,* 109(35), 14158–63.

Chevallier, A. (2000). *Encyclopedia of Herbal Medicine.* New York: Dorling Kindersley.

Clark, R. (1971). *Einstein.* New York: World Pub. Co.

de Vries, M, et al. (2013, May). Combining deliberation and intuition in patient decision support. *Patient Education and Counseling,* 91(2), 154–60.

Dioxins and their effects on human health. (2014, Jun). World Health Organization. Retrieved from http://www.who.int/mediacentre/factsheets/fs225/en

Einstein, A, & Calaprice, A. (2000). *The Expanded Quotable Einstein.* Princeton, NJ: Princeton University Press.

Espinosa, S. (2014). The therapeutic role of the practitioner's heart in classical medicine and modern medical science: A critical literature review. *The European Journal of Oriental Medicine*, 7(5), 18–25.

Gaynor, ML. (2002). *The Healing Power of Sound*. Boston: Shambhala.

Gopinath, B, et al. (2011). Dietary antioxidant intake is associated with the prevalence but not incidence of age-related hearing loss. *J. Nutr Health Aging*, 15(10), 896–900.

Hay, L. (1984). *Heal Your Body*. Carlsbad, CA: Hay House, Inc.

Hekmat A, Saboury AA, & Moosavi-Movahedi AA. (2013, Feb). The toxic effects of mobile phone radiofrequency (940 MHz) on the structure of calf thymus DNA. *Ecotoxicol Environ Saf*, 88, 35–41.

Isenman, L. (2009). Trusting your gut, among other things: Digestive enzyme secretion, intuition, and the history of science. *Found Science*, 14, 315–29.

Larsson, SC, et al. (2006, Nov). Consumption of sugar and sugar-sweetened foods and the risk of pancreatic cancer in a prospective study. *Am J Clin Nutr*, 85(5), 1171–6.

Le Prell, CG, Hughes, LF, & Miller, JM. (2007). Free radical scavengers vitamins A, C, and E plus magnesium reduce noise trauma. *Free Radic Biol Med*, 42(9), 1454–63.

May, EC, et al. (2005, Aug). Anomalous anticipatory skin conductance response to acoustic stimuli: experimental results and speculation about a mechanism. *Journal of Alternative & Complementary Medicine*, 11(4), 695–702.

McCown, RL. (2012, Feb). Farmers use intuition to reinvent analytic decision support for managing seasonal climatic variability. *Agricultural Systems*, 106(1), 33–45.

McCraty, R, Atkinson, M, & Bradley, RT. (2004). Electrophysiological evidence of intuition: Part 1. The surprising role of the heart. *Journal of Alternative and Complementary Medicine*, 10(1), 133–43.

———. (2004). Electrophysiological evidence of intuition: Part 2. A system-wide process? *Journal of Alternative and Complementary Medicine*, 10(2), 325–36.

Mills, S, & Bone, K. (2000). *Principles and Practice of Phytotherapy*. Edinburgh: Churchill Livingstone.

Murray, M, & Pizzorno, J. (1998). *Encyclopedia of Natural Medicine* (2nd ed.). Roseville, CA: Prima Publishing.

Myers, DG. (2002). *Intuition: Its Powers and Perils*. New Haven, CT: Yale University Press.

Quaglino, D. (2004). The effect on rat thymocytes of the simultaneous *in vivo* exposure to 50-Hz electric and magnetic field and to continuous light. *The Scientific World Journal*, 4(S2), 91–9.

Radin, D. (2009). *The Conscious Universe: The Scientific Truth of Psychic Phenomena*. San Francisco: HarperOne Publishers.

Remmers, C, Topolinski, S, Dietrich, DE, & Michalak, J. (2014, Oct 11). Impaired intuition in patients with major depressive disorder. *The British Journal of Clinical Psychology,* 54(2), 200–13.

Rowland, IR. (1991). *Nutrition, Toxicity, and Cancer.* London: Taylor & Francis.

Silva, C, et al. (2014). Effects of high-fat diets from different sources on serum and thymus lipid profile: study in an experimental model. *Endocr Metab Immune Disord Drug Targets,* 14(2), 77–83.

Sokolovic, D, et al. (2013). Melatonin protects rat thymus against oxidative stress caused by exposure to microwaves and modulates proliferation/apoptosis of thymocytes. *Gen Physiol Biophys,* 32(1), 79–90.

Spankovich, C. (2013, Jun). Healthy diets, healthy hearing: National Health and Nutrition Examination Survey, 1999–2002. *Intl J of Audiology,* 52(6), 369–76.

Spottiswoode, SJP, & May, EC. (2003). Skin conductance prestimulus response: Analyses, artifacts, and a pilot study. *Journal of Scientific Exploration,* 17(4), 617–41.

Suzuki, S. (1969). *Nurtured by Love: A New Approach to Education* (1st ed.). New York: Exposition Press.

Takotsubo cardiomyopathy (broken-heart syndrome). (2010, Nov 1). *Harvard Women's Health Watch, Harvard Health Publications.* Retrieved from http://www.health.harvard. edu/heart-health/takotsubo-cardiomyopathy-broken-heart-syndrome

Trickey, R. (2003). *Women, Hormones, and the Menstrual Cycle* (2nd ed.). Crows Nest, Australia: Allen and Unwin.

Veile, A, et al. (2012). Infant growth and the thymus: Data from two South American native societies. *Am J of Hum Bio,* 24(6), 768–75.

Virtue, D. (1994). *Constant Craving.* Carlsbad, CA: Hay House, Inc.

———. (2001). *The Care and Feeding of Indigo Children.* Carlsbad, CA: Hay House, Inc.

———. (2015). *Don't Let Anything Dull Your Sparkle.* Carlsbad, CA: Hay House, Inc.

Virtue, D, & Reeves, R. (2014). *Angel Detox.* Carlsbad, CA: Hay House, Inc.

Wood, M. (1997). *The Book of Herbal Wisdom.* Berkeley, CA: North Atlantic Books.

———. (2008). *The Earthwise Herbal: A Complete Guide to Old World Medicinal Plants.* Berkeley, CA: North Atlantic Books.

———. (2009). *The Earthwise Herbal: A Complete Guide to New World Medicinal Plants.* Berkeley, CA: North Atlantic Books.

ABOUT THE AUTHORS

Doreen Virtue holds three university degrees in counseling psychology. A former psychotherapist who specialized in eating disorders, she developed an interest in nutrition in childhood, as her mother and vegetarian father would serve healthful meals. As a lifelong clairvoyant, Doreen has received information about which foods to eat and which to avoid to increase intuition. One hundred percent vegan since 1996, she changed her diet to follow her guidance and was rewarded with good health and high intuition as a result.

Doreen is the author of several books about nutrition, including *The Yo-Yo Diet Syndrome, Eating in the Light* (with Becky Black), *Constant Craving, The Art of Raw Living Food* (with Jenny Ross), *Angel Detox* (with Robert Reeves), and *Don't Let Anything Dull Your Sparkle*. Doreen has appeared on radio and television worldwide, including CNN, *Oprah,* and *The View*, and in magazines and newspapers internationally. She hosts a weekly call-in show on HayHouseRadio .com® and teaches online video classes through her website: Angel Therapy.com.

ANGEL THERAPY®

Robert Reeves, N.D., is an accredited naturopath who blends his herbal medicine and nutrition training with his psychic and mediumship abilities. He has a strong connection to the angels and to the natural world, believing that nature holds Divine healing properties. Robert loves creating new smoothies and juices, which he has found greatly enhances his intuition.

Robert teaches online workshops, with participants from over 30 countries, which help people develop their own spiritual gifts. He has developed a range of vibrational essences focusing on crystal and angel energy, which are currently available as aura sprays. Robert is co-author, with Doreen, of *Flower Therapy, Flower Therapy Oracle Cards, Angel Detox,* and *Living Pain-Free.*

For more information about Robert, please visit: www.Robert Reeves.com.au or facebook.com/RobertReevesNaturopath.

Hay House Titles of Related Interest

YOU CAN HEAL YOUR LIFE, the movie,
starring Louise Hay & Friends
(available as a 1-DVD program and an expanded 2-DVD set)
Watch the trailer at: www.LouiseHayMovie.com

THE SHIFT, the movie,
starring Dr. Wayne W. Dyer
(available as a 1-DVD program and an expanded 2-DVD set)
Watch the trailer at: www.DyerMovie.com

*CRAZY SEXY JUICE: 100+ Simple Juice, Smoothie &
Nut Milk Recipes to Supercharge Your Health,* by Kris Carr

*HEALING WITH RAW FOODS: Your Guide to Unlocking
Vibrant Health Through Living Cuisine,* by Jenny Ross

*LOVING YOURSELF TO GREAT HEALTH: Thoughts & Food—the
Ultimate Diet,* by Louise Hay, Ahlea Khadro, and Heather Dane

*MEALS THAT HEAL INFLAMMATION: Embrace Healthy Living
and Eliminate Pain, One Meal at a Time,* by Julie Daniluk, R.H.N.

THE PLANTPLUS DIET SOLUTION: Personalized Nutrition for Life,
by Joan Borysenko, Ph.D.

*REAL FOOD REVOLUTION: Healthy Eating, Green Groceries, and the
Return of the American Family Farm,* by Congressman Tim Ryan

All of the above are available at your local bookstore,
or may be ordered by contacting Hay House (see next page).

We hope you enjoyed this Hay House book. If you'd like to receive our online catalog featuring additional information on Hay House books and products, or if you'd like to find out more about the Hay Foundation, please contact:

Hay House, Inc., P.O. Box 5100, Carlsbad, CA 92018-5100
(760) 431-7695 or (800) 654-5126
(760) 431-6948 (fax) or (800) 650-5115 (fax)
www.hayhouse.com® • www.hayfoundation.org

Published and distributed in Australia by: Hay House Australia Pty. Ltd., 18/36 Ralph St., Alexandria NSW 2015
Phone: 612-9669-4299 • *Fax:* 612-9669-4144 • www.hayhouse.com.au

Published and distributed in the United Kingdom by: Hay House UK, Ltd., Astley House, 33 Notting Hill Gate, London W11 3JQ
Phone: 44-20-3675-2450 • *Fax:* 44-20-3675-2451 • www.hayhouse.co.uk

Published and distributed in the Republic of South Africa by: Hay House SA (Pty), Ltd., P.O. Box 990, Witkoppen 2068
info@hayhouse.co.za • www.hayhouse.co.za

Published in India by: Hay House Publishers India, Muskaan Complex, Plot No. 3, B-2, Vasant Kunj, New Delhi 110 070
Phone: 91-11-4176-1620 • *Fax:* 91-11-4176-1630 • www.hayhouse.co.in

Distributed in Canada by: Raincoast Books, 2440 Viking Way, Richmond, B.C. V6V 1N2
Phone: 1-800-663-5714 • *Fax:* 1-800-565-3770 • www.raincoast.com

Take Your Soul on a Vacation

Visit www.HealYourLife.com® to regroup, recharge, and reconnect with your own magnificence. Featuring blogs, mind-body-spirit news, and life-changing wisdom from Louise Hay and friends.

Visit www.HealYourLife.com today!